GROOMING YOUR HORSE

GROOMING
YOUR HORSE

Neale Haley

SOUTH BRUNSWICK AND NEW YORK: A. S. BARNES AND COMPANY
LONDON: THOMAS YOSELOFF LTD

© 1974 by A. S. Barnes and Co., Inc.

A. S. Barnes and Co., Inc.
Cranbury, New Jersey 08512

Thomas Yoseloff Ltd
108 New Bond Street
London W1Y OQX, England

Library of Congress Cataloging in Publication Data

Haley, Neale.
    Grooming your horse.

    1. Horses—Grooming. I. Title.
SF285.3.H33   636.1'08'33   73-143
ISBN 0-498-01280-8

This book is dedicated to my favorite aunt, Laura L. Adams,
who is my most enthusiastic admirer.

Contents

Acknowledgments

Horsemen think grooming is automatic, because they have done it so often. Most of them could probably do it in their sleep. But there are so many small details for a beginner to learn, and even more for the person who wants to enter a horse show. I have tried to include as many as possible, taking the information from experts all over the country.

At Camp Longacres, everyone knows grooming is not automatic. Each year it is taught from the ground up—hoofs up— to hundreds of children. Tom Kranz, the director, made this book possible by making it easy for me to take over a thousand pictures of campers in every stage of grooming. Special appreciation goes to Jacqueline Kranz who stood by to help find the angles for photos, requisitioned counselors from her staff for aid with children and posing, and gave advice through each phase of the writing.

Understanding a horse is not automatic, either, even for someone who has ridden for years. Captain Alexi Erlanger always stresses this point for dressage riders. I also appreciate comments made by Joe Fargis, a former member of the United States Equestrian team.

The horse show world is full of glamor. Nearly every rider wants to taste it sometime. Grooming, for both English and Western riders, is an important step toward winning. For his advice on preparing a horse for a Western horse show, I am most appreciative to Mr. James I. Wilson of East Aurora, New York. Ginger Trautwein, who has ridden in both English and Western shows, helped me with comparisons. As ever, both Doug and Kim Haley stepped forth with ideas for the book, about both showing and everyday riding.

Only when you come to take pictures of how to do something do you realize how different each phase of it is. So many people helped make the photographs possible. Marjorie Schattauer of East Aurora, New York, spent hours outlining the types of pictures needed—thereby

9

sharing with me the idea for the basic form of the book. Nor did she stop there. While I took the pictures, she moved horses (which is not always as easy as it sounds) and children (which can be even harder), and came up with brushes and sponges and bits of cotton just when they were needed for the next picture. My thanks to the Saddler in Wilton, Connecticut, for their unusual display of grooming tools.

It's not easy, either, to find horses when you want them. I'm told there are 40,000 of them in Fairfield County, and it seems now as if I found the hidden ones. Susie and Renna Martin, Leslie Castle, and Martha Maynard offered theirs. Martha also helped with explanations of mud knots and braiding tails; she even phoned me from the stable with her horse standing backside to while she braided and talked. Adults also offered their horses, and my thanks go to Judy Schmidt of Greenwich, Connecticut, Mike Donnery of Greenwich, Mary Reams Maynard of Greenwich, and Ann Pierce of Cos Cob.

Ox Ridge Hunt Club of Darien, Connecticut arranged for me to take the pictures on clipping a horse's winter coat. (And the horse let me use flashbulbs, but it is difficult to thank him properly.) Donald D. Cornell did the clipping in a most cooperative and professional manner.

Round Hill Stables of Greenwich also made picture-taking easy for me. Teddy Wahl enhanced the afternoon with memories of the past and bits about grooming.

Thanks, too, to Bob Trostli for his heroic efforts in getting out the book.

Special thanks go to all the campers at Longacres and all the children and adults from Greenwich, Cos Cob, and New Canaan to San Luis Obispo, California, who posed for ideas in photography about grooming a horse.

To my artist, Margery Reeves Kinley of Greenwich, Connecticut, all horsemen who care about horses say thank you. And thanks, also, to Diane Foster of Hamburg, New York, for her two drawings.

10

Part I

WHAT GROOMING IS

1

Why Groom Your Own Horse?

Dominion—the feeling of being a king on an Arabian who leaps to obey your slightest whim—is a joy in riding. One of the most important reasons for grooming your own horse is to get this dominion, to establish your authority. You control him easily in the stall. He becomes accustomed to your voice, your odor, your way of moving. He expects to do what you ask. Your touch anywhere on his body is accepted. His trust in you grows. You are giving him care in a form he enjoys, so that he associates a pleasant feeling with being with you. This feeling carries over to riding hours. Not only do you know him better because you groom him; he knows you better too.

A horse includes in his circle of "friends" the one who feeds him, the one who grooms him, and the one who rides him. Why share your horse with someone else who will have equal stature in his eyes? You can be the one all-important person in his life.

There's a togetherness in riding. You can have the same sharing feeling in the stall. Grooming helps you recognize how your horse sees things, how he reacts to the world around him; it makes you conscious of his universe. When you ride, you suddenly see things through your horse's eyes. He broadens the scope of your vision. Riding becomes a time to share motion, sounds, and eagerness with an animal you know well. Your companionship grows.

In the old days, a gentleman refused to soil his hands with grooming. A job like that was below his dignity. He *thought* he rode just as well without knowing anything about his horse's life in the half-darkness

In the old days gentlemen rode horses and someone else groomed them.

of the stable. If you expect to understand horses, don't let this old-fashioned attitude cling to you.

At the stable where your horse lives someone else may give your horse an expert's care. Riders in classes may come to the mounting block without an idea of what goes on behind the scenes. Do not join the throng. Learn everything you can about your horse in his off hours. And if you don't own a horse, but hope to some day, now is the time to find out about grooming.

Perhaps you want a character change in your horse. Groom him. My daughter's Morgan, when we first bought him, seemed devoid of all personality traits except selfishness. What he wanted, he got, either by stubborness or naughtiness. Even though she rode him every day, he never paid any attention to what she asked. Tug, pull, yank, kick, and he still plunged into the undergrowth. But she loved him anyhow. Finally she started taking care of him herself. Within a week, he paused a moment before he bucked, but he still bucked. At the end of a month, a spark shone in his eyes when he saw her coming. He didn't buck as high. Finally he would do almost anything for her, on the ground or in the saddle, although he remained as infuriating as ever with anyone else.

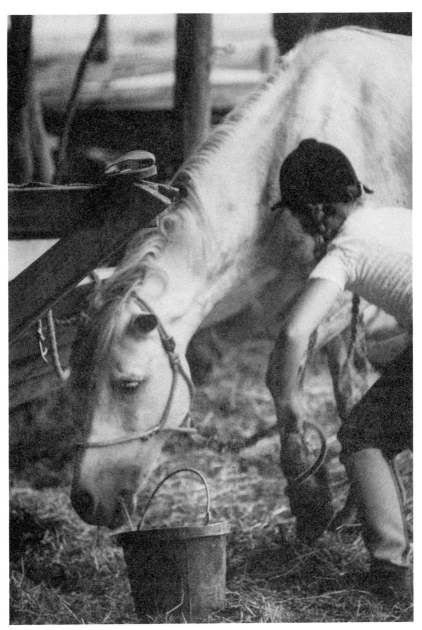

If you want his cooperation, you'd better get to know him in his stall.

No one cares as much about your horse's health as you do. Even though someone else could probably get rid of the grease and other body wastes on his skin just as well as you, you care more. *You* won't miss that hot feeling in his leg, or the bump on his side that wasn't there the day before. You'll notice if he suddenly develops an odd habit and you will hunt for the cause.

Deb discovered, after her horse had been left with friends for a few weeks, that they had trouble bridling him. As soon as she groomed him —something she did the moment she got him home—he just about talked to her. As her brush touched behind his ears, up shot his head. She looked at his ears. "Well, no wonder . . ." she said, as she saw how flies had infested them. Every day, for many days, she rubbed cocoa butter in his ears until the flies gave up.

Most horses are sensitive about something. Grooming teaches you the little things that bother them. This extra bit of knowledge makes you ride a little more cautiously or kindly or firmly. When you understand your horse, you will ride him better than someone who hasn't worked with him in the stall. And often this knowledge carries over to the way you ride other horses.

Pherion was sensitive about everything, but especially about being touched. The best way to teach a rider just *how* sensitive Pherion felt was to let the rider groom the horse. By the time someone had managed to brush Pherion all over—which took gentleness, a kind voice, and patience—the rider never forgot to keep his heels out of Pherion's sides during a ride.

A young horse develops his trust in you while you are working around him in the stall. This trust becomes the foundation for all of his basic training.

Grooming is a key to understanding the reflexes, sociability, and likes of your horse. Horses are curious about everything. Your horse won't take his groom for granted. He is curious about him. He gets to know him. He reacts to him, to *his* moods and sociability. How much better for your horse to get to know you than a stranger.

All experts agree that grooming is an important aspect of getting to know your horse. A horseman is always seeking what Captain Alexi Erlanger, an expert in dressage, calls "perfect understanding between horse and rider." This is the only sure way to become an expert in riding. How do you attain it? Captain Erlanger says, "It certainly helps if you begin to untack your own horse, rub him off, brush him and, best of all, take over his entire care."

If you are training a foal, it is ever so important to do his grooming yourself.

2

What's Important About Grooming?

Grooming is make-him-beautiful time. It's the way to have your horse's tail flow, his mane fluff, his coat shine, his feet dance, and his blood leap around eagerly under his skin. It is also touch-him-tenderly time. Each time you groom you ask with your hands, "Does anything hurt, my friend?"

It is important that you groom him often, every day if you can, and certainly every day if he works. Even a horse running free in pasture, with the wind in his face and his coat cleaned by rolling and rain, needs your care: his hoofs must be cleaned every day.

It's important to rub hard with your brush. Use all your muscle and your back. Scrubbing a horse is a bit like scrubbing a floor. Once-over-lightly makes him look better, but it leaves the real dirt clinging under the surface where it can itch and make him sore. One member of a pony club had a problem pony. He liked mud so much that he sought it out every chance he had—and he was white. If his mistress went lightly over his coat with a small-sized pony club brush so that she did not disturb the hairs underneath, her pony looked fine. But once the dirt was ruffled even a little, he looked as filthy as he was. Once that happened, she had to get a stiff dandy brush, hold it in both hands, and work on him for days to get him clean.

The size you've grown doesn't have a great deal to do with how clean you get a horse. (It will only affect how *long* it takes.) At horse care in the wee morning hours at summer camp, I often watch a score of seven- to- twelve-year-olds grooming their horses, each one giving loving effort to the horse of his choice. They work so hard they soon shed jackets and sweaters until the fence of the corral looks like a clothesline. They get their horses clean, and they do it in about half an hour, which is all the time they have before the breakfast bell rings.

The time of day you take your brush in hand is not so important. Just don't choose a time when the school bus is about to arrive, or Mom wants help getting dinner, or it is too dark to see. If you groom at the end of the day, be sure your horse is not weary from a long ride. Give him a breather while he eats his hay; then groom him.

Though the sun glints warm over his pasture and the wind comes cool off the mountains, remember him. A sharp rock can cut him, a bit of glass carelessly thrown can injure him. Look at his feet each day. When you bring him in, you can groom him any time of day—except graining time.

Graining time is the highlight of your horse's day. He is too excited to be patient if you try to groom him then. Besides, you want all his attention on digesting those oats. They give a gloss to his coat, too.

Strange as it may seem, daily grooming is the easiest way to keep your horse clean. If you skip him one day, you'll more than double the grooming time for the next day. If you try just once a week, dirt accumulates, his hair mats, and grease glues itself to his skin.

Sometimes you want your horse to be extra-special clean. Maybe you are going to a horse show. Maybe it is a pony club rally. Perhaps you are meeting a friend for lunch. In Ireland horses are groomed specially on sale day. That is the only time some of the grooms on stud farms really groom the stallions: when the owners want to sell them.

Your special grooming means more to you than a regular grooming. You've learned how easily passersby say, "Oh what a beautiful horse!" You know it takes even more work to have another horseman say, "Your horse sparkles today!" Best of all is show-ring clean, when he is so well groomed a white glove touching his coat stays white.

Few campers at Longacres could clean a horse the way Mitzi did. Mitzi seldom said much, though she smiled often. When she worked, she did it with her whole heart and body. When she cleaned a horse, she did more than put her back into it; she put her love into it, too. Every morning at 6:45, you could see Mitzi sitting on the roots of a giant oak tree at the top of the path that led to the stable. No camper could pass the oak tree until a counselor came with the tack house key. So Mitzi waited. Often the dew lay on the trailing vines that dipped into the ravine spread out at her feet. Sometimes you could see Mitzi's breath on the air, it was so cold. Sometimes the rain had turned the path into a stream. But Mitzi was there, looking up the hill toward the stable where her horse waited.

The first day Mitzi came to camp, the counselor who checked to see if the horses were clean expected to find fault with Mitzi's grooming. After all, new campers always left dirt on the pastern, or inside the legs, or behind the horse's knees. Not Mitzi. Her horse's coat felt soft as a snake's skin. His tail lay silky against his legs. His hoofs could have walked on the kitchen floor without leaving a mark. It had taken Mitzi forty-five minutes to accomplish this miracle—for miracle it seemed to the cluster of campers around her. After that, Mitzi performed the same miracle every morning.

Any camper from Horseman's Club at Longacres will tell you it usually takes at least a couple of hours to groom a horse perfectly. A Horseman's Club member knows: he had to do it. That's the price of admission to the club.

Sometimes you will have to spend longer than other times grooming.

On those mornings when you cannot rub the sleep from your eyes, it takes longer, somehow. Grooming is harder when the horse has a winter coat. If he rolled happily in the mud the day before, you pay for it. One of the hardest times to get him clean is after he has been in pasture for weeks and weeks. His croup seems to have sprouted dirt.

You want him to be gentle and quiet, willing and obedient. It is such a delight to own a horse who holds down his head while you clean his ears and lifts his tail to the side while you groom behind his legs. It is so much easier to clean his feet if *he* holds them up. How do you teach your horse to act this way? Earn his trust while you groom him. Then he wants to make it easy for you. He learns your routine. Gradually he becomes trained to help and obey you.

You cannot be like Gretchen was the first day she groomed a horse. Gretchen said she'd clean Pep because he was small and she liked buckskins. Usually Pep paid no attention to children coming into his stall. Gretchen was different. He noticed her. She squeezed as far away from him as the edge of his stall permitted. Squeamishly she touched his shoulder with the currycomb. Pep jumped. Gretchen squeaked. Pep jumped again. Then they both tried to duck out of the stall as fast as they could.

Whether your horse is a pure breed or just a horse, whether he is pony-sized or a Percheron, he needs you at grooming time. You'll both gain more from the time together if you come to him with a grin. Sing if you like. Talk sweet talk or just talk. He likes it any way.

3

Grooming Tools

"Brushes are what a person wants to have. They are a personal thing," said a successful show rider. "Around here a cactus fiber cloth is popular, especially with the Arabs [owners of Arabian horses]. It works better than a dandy brush and gives a real good shine."

This brings up a basic argument about grooming tools. Some horsemen argue that only a brush, and a soft brush at that, should be used on a horse—they will also use a rag, which can be even softer. These men argue that a currycomb is the lazy man's tool and is hard on a horse. How do you know? Ask your horse. If he has a tender skin and you start to use a stiff brush or a currycomb on him, he'll tell you fast enough. His ears will go back, he will twitch and stomp and move away from your hand.

For most horses you will use three basic grooming tools: a currycomb, a stiff brush, and a soft brush.

You will need a stiff brush. A rice brush has very stiff bristles. Some brushes with synthetic bristles can be stiff. All the stiff brushes go under the name of *dandy brush*.

A softer brush is used at the end of your grooming. It gets off the dust, shines his coat. You use it in the tender spots, too, where a stiff brush might hurt your horse. These softer brushes are usually called *body brushes*. Many body brushes have long bristles on them, but the bristles are not as stiff as on a dandy brush. There is also a body brush with short bristles an inch or two long. This is less likely to hurt your horse than a dandy brush because the bristles are short and closely packed in order not to cut deeply into his coat.

A bristle brush gets deeper into the hair than a fiber brush does. The

22

Which ones do you buy? These. You'll want a stiff brush. The softest brush is used to dampen the mane and tail and for a thin-skinned horse. It is good for sensitive spots, too. A rubber currycomb is the one made for horses. A plastic brush with plastic bristles is good for manes and tails—better even than a mane-and-tail comb. And it gets into a thick winter coat in a way a rubber currycomb never could. A sweat scraper with a curvy blade takes the water off.

bristles wear down, but fibers flatten down and when they do the brush won't penetrate a horse's coat. So for tough spots and a tough skin, you use a bristle brush. For tender spots and tender horses, choose a fiber one.

"I go through three body brushes a year," Susie Martin said, shaking her head in exasperation as she brushed the legs of her Lippizaner. Most horsemen sigh with Susie about brushes. They have learned to watch the shape of their brushes. A dandy brush's bristles grow shorter instead of longer with passing days. The shorter they grow the harder they dig into your horse's skin. The flatter the bristles on your body brush, the less good they do. When a brush ceases to work the way it should you will have to buy a new one. Yet, horsemen love brushes. If you peek into the cupboard where most horsemen keep their tools, you will almost surely find some beautiful ones.

Besides brushes, you will need a currycomb, sponges, rags, mane brush, comb, and hoofpicks. There are two types of currycombs: rubber and metal. The rubber one is for your horse; the metal one is to clean your brush. If you own a metal one, never, never use it on your horse. What about his thick winter coat? Use a plastic brush, the type that works so well to comb out manes and tails. You can also use a sweat scraper with a rough edge to comb out winter hair.

Sweat scrapers come in two kinds. One has a curved, flexible, bendy shape that goes into the curves of his body and the upper part of his legs. There's a stiff kind, too, that is slightly curved. Either one will wipe off your horse's sweat or lather and wipe him dry after a bath.

A rubbing cloth is any rag you use for wiping your horse. A good one can be made from that old blanket you washed so many times, or from the salt sack shipped from the feed mill. It's even better than a sponge because you can wash it and boil it and use it over and over again.

If you are on a tight budget, you can make do with improvised grooming tools. A scrub brush will serve as a dandy brush. Rags will work well in place of sponges. An old brush of yours or your dog's will straighten out your horse's mane and tail. A screwdriver can be turned into a hoof pick by curving it into a U. Even a sweat scraper can be home-made: take a fine-toothed hacksaw blade and tape both ends for handles. Old crankcase oil will keep his hoofs from drying out, and it can be put on with a rag.

Keep track of your grooming tools. It isn't just that they cost so much, but that, left in the wrong place, they can harm a horse. Leslie Castle had been using the hoof pick. Afterwards she put it in what she considered a safe place and promptly forgot the place. Half an hour later I saw her looking around frantically for something.

"I can't find the hoof pick," she said, that note of strain in her voice that made you look quickly at her horse's feet to see if it were there.

"It's on the fence," I said.

"Where?" Her eye ran the length of the fence.

"Under Decision's neck, maybe?"

She made a grab under her horse's neck just as he stretched it to full length to reach the grass on the far side.

Care of your grooming tools includes a bath for your brushes about once a week. Have a small box or ledge for your hoofpicks, or a hook where they are secure. They are more easily lost than any item in your tool kit. You should have one folding hoof pick. Whenever you ride it should go along in your pocket. Sticks just won't work as well as hoof picks in digging out stones from your horse's hoof in the middle of a ride.

One last tool, which really isn't a grooming tool, should be in your box of tools all the time: a sharp jackknife. It can mean life to a horse, your horse. Sometimes you need to cut a rope in a terrible hurry. Who can say why or how horses can get into so much trouble with ropes? But they can. Once caught, only a knife will get them free before they strangle or break a leg.

Look at all your brushes and tools and feel proud. Remember, then, it is the effort you put behind them that gets your horse clean. The tools make it easier, that's all. The energy you spend grooming your horse is one of the best gifts you can give him. It is love in action.

4
How to Use
Your Grooming Tools

You begin with a curry, working a brush along behind it. When his whole body is finished, you give him a final shine with rag or rubbing cloth, your hands or a soft brush. Use a soft brush with long hairs as your polishing cloth, your face brush, and your be-nice-to-horse's legs brush. Off comes the dandruff, away flies the dust. When everything else is done, take the body brush in hand to give your horse a shine. Make long, sweeping strokes all over his body. A hoof pick, with its curved tip, is only used on the bottoms of his feet. A sweat scraper is used in the direction of his hair to scrape excess water out of his coat after a bath.

A rubber currycomb is kind to your horse. Round and round in circles it goes. Rub against the way his hair grows. Bang out the curry on your heel, or stoop to tap it on the floor. Do it often. You're supposed to hold the curry in your left hand on the near side and in your right hand when you clean the off side.

The dandy brush—the stiff one—follows the curry. It whisks off dust and grime, and loosens hair stirred up by the currycomb. Use short, hard strokes, moving it the way his hair grows. Flip up the strokes at the end to flick the dust off. Lean on that brush! Make it work.

Every three or four strokes wipe off the dandy brush on your currycomb.

5

Ticklish Spots

A horse lets you know if you tickle him. He may flinch. His skin may ripple as if he were trembling or shooing away a fly. He may pick up a hoof as if to say, "Don't you know that tickles?" The surest sign is ears laid flat.

Ticklish spots are the sensitive places on a horse. The first one you are likely to hit when you groom is between his forelegs. He's just as sensitive between his rear legs. His flanks, the area along his sides in front of his rear legs, is another one of those ticklish spots.

He has tender areas, too, where a hard brush or currycomb can actually hurt him. You know simply by thinking about it that a horse doesn't like to be hit in the face. You should be gentle with his ears too, knowing that even a fly biting him there makes him toss his head in anguish. Any place where the bones are close to the surface of the skin is tender, just the way your shins are. The bones are close to the skin on the lower half of his legs. You don't use a currycomb or stiff brush below his knees on his forelegs, or below his hocks (those are the big bones that stick out behind) on his rear legs. His pasterns, the joints just above his hoofs, must be treated with care too.

Whenever a horse might be ticklish, keep the currycomb and stiff brush away. If you hit an especially muddy spot, you may need to use a stiffer brush, but remember you are using it and go easy. A sponge and water often cleans such a spot best of all.

Grooming is one way to help keep your horse's legs sound. There are two spots to watch on his legs: behind the pasterns and the bottoms of his feet. Don't be afraid to groom his legs just because they are sensitive. Legs are too important to do them lightly.

Soft brushes for tender spots, a harder brush for the muddy ones.

You don't need to be afraid of his hoofs. Most horses won't kick when you are grooming them. Even if you hurt your horse by accident, he will forgive you if you say you're sorry and pat him properly. He understands the tone, if not the words. Just watch those ticklish spots.

Suppose he does pick up a hoof. It's likely he is after an itch on his belly. But if his ears go back and he gives you a nasty look at the same time, look out!

The closer you are to his hind legs when you go around him, the safer you are. Even if he kicks you, all he does is bump you with his

If you stand at the side of your horse, his hoofs can't reach you.

big bones. Stand a couple of feet behind him, let his hoofs pick up momentum as they lift into the air, and he'll wallop you. Remember he can kick forward with a rear hoof, too. Keep a hand on his leg as you clean it and you'll feel it if he picks up a hoof.

Denah, a seven-year-old, stood half as high as her horse. Every day when the counselor at camp checked to see if her horse felt clean, his legs were dirty.

"He picks up his feet if I try to brush his legs," Denah said.

"Then wait until he puts down his foot," the counselor said. "He can't stand on three legs forever."

After that Denah could often be seen watching a raised hoof until it touched the ground. She would get in a quick rub before the leg lifted again. The horse tired of holding up his foot sooner than Denah tired of waiting. His legs got cleaned.

Some horses are sensitive on their stomachs. Test your horse by using the currycomb gently there. If he doesn't give you a "watch out" look, you can go ahead.

A horse may have his own peculiar ticklish spots. Jiggers's "funny bone" was behind his ears. How he tossed his head whenever Sammy touched him there!

"So you want me to be careful," Sammy would say.

Jiggers would nod emphatically.

Sammy, so short he had to stand on tip-toe to reach Jiggers's neck

A damp sponge will take off dirt on his belly, even if he is sensitive there. You can use a sponge on muddy legs, too.

at all, brushed gently. "I know you'll never get to *like* getting your neck clean," Sammy would say. "I hate to wash mine too." Jiggers finally did come to trust Sammy enough to allow him to clean his neck thoroughly. His ears stayed half-back, however, warning Sammy to watch what he was doing just the same.

You'll find, as Sammy did, that a bit of talking helps get the brush over the ticklish spots.

6

A Lick-and-a-Promise Grooming

Give your horse a lick-and-a-promise grooming before you ride. You may only have a few minutes, but take those minutes and use them well.

You may be the kind of horseman who likes to groom at the day's end, when night is soft beyond the stable and fresh hay makes the air sweet with its scent. You like the quietness then, with all your other work done. This is your special time with your horse. You may be one of those riders who believes it is wisest to groom a horse after his ride, when all the sweat is bothering him, and he is dirty from the trail. Either way, before you put tack on your horse, there are five places you should never miss cleaning.

Saddles sit on withers and backs, and every time you post or sit to a jog, the saddle squeaks a bit and wiggles a bit and slips a bit under your weight. As it moves it rubs the tufts of hair beneath the blankets or pad. Dirt lost in the hair, dirt close to the skin, is like sandpaper to your horse.

Girths shove the skin around on your horse's belly. They tug at the skin behind his foreleg, bunch it up, stretch it out. Where the girth touches and where it ruffles the flesh next to his foreleg, brush your horse smooth and soft. That's girth-sore territory.

The bridle looks well on him. Does it hide dirt behind his ears? Does it rub his nose or brow where you forgot to brush? Under his throat the throatlatch can gather in lather if he gets hot. If there's a curb chain, it should be clean under his lips too.

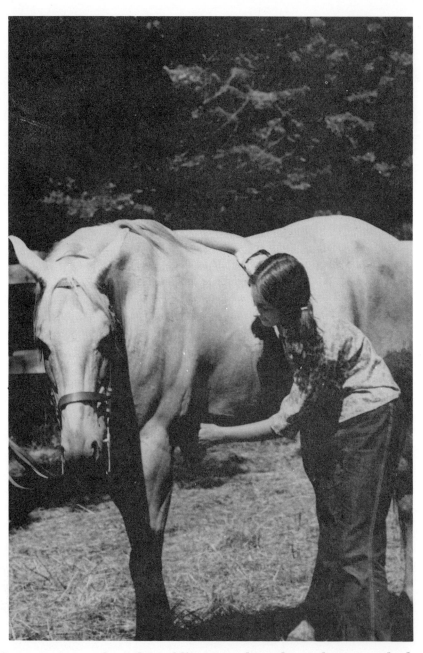

Spots to clean: where the saddle goes, where the girth goes, and where the bridle goes.

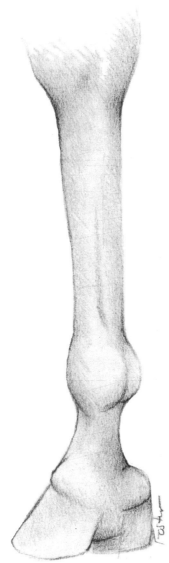

Then there's his all-important legs. Mud and manure get stomped or kicked or climb into the pastern dip just above his hoof. A horse gets sore and goes lame if his pasterns are not cleaned. Finally, clean all four hoofs.

7

Touch-Up Grooming

You did your best to bring him home cool. You always walk at the beginning and end of your ride. If he just wouldn't be so eager about getting home for his oats, he'd be cooler. Oh, well, so you walk him a while. Now? A quick check with a hand between his front legs. That's the last place he gets cool, so if he's dry and cool there, he's ready for a drink and a rest. No heat? Good!

A brush-off on the saddle area. That takes care of any sweat worked up there. As a girl I once put a horse away without rubbing the saddle area. When the owner of the stable said, "Did you wipe off any sweat marks?" I had to admit I hadn't.

"But there wasn't a brush," I added.

She was a patient woman, usually, but this time she bristled. "A burlap bag will do," she said, "or if there's nothing else, a handful of straw. But *never put a horse away without rubbing him down.*"

Somehow that is the kind of lesson you remember.

A horse sweats under his girth. Especially in winter, if his coat is thick, he needs a wipe-off underneath.

A burlap bag makes a rag. Always dry off the saddle and girth areas, where the throatlatch rubs and the brow band pulls, and at the corners of his mouth where the bit rubs.

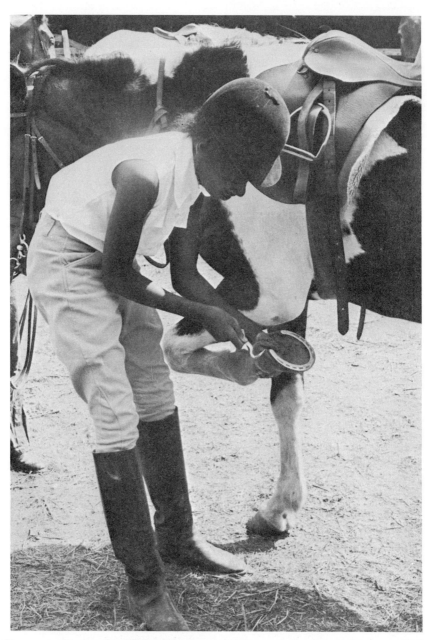

Clean out his hoofs. Check his shoes. Can you imagine waiting until the next day with a stone in your foot?

8

The *Musts* for a Well-Groomed Horse

The tall Saddlebred squealed at the pony on the other side of the fence. They were friends.

Ellen Grimm looked affectionately at her pony Jacques and said, "He never acts up for me. Only when someone else is on him does he get excited. But I don't give him much grain." She held out her cupped hand. "Just that much, and only at night. You know ponies really don't need grain."

Her friend, Leslie Castle, didn't seem a bit jealous. She had been trying for weeks to put weight on the Saddlebred. "He was skinny when he came here," she said. "So now he gets 12 quarts a day."

Your horse needs the right amount of good feed if he is to have the beautiful look that makes you proud after a grooming.

Pepper, though he was only a pony, bullied the mare, Ancona, who shared his large corral. Susie could always be sure Ancona had her share of the hay when she stood by to keep guard, but sometimes she couldn't be there. One afternoon Susie filled the stable with Ancona's hay, shut the door tightly, and warned the whole family to keep the door shut so Pepper wouldn't get inside. Then she left.

Pepper had other ideas. Twenty minutes later he had disappeared. Susie's mother looked worriedly at the empty corral. Renna hurried out to see what had happened. She found Pepper quickly enough. He had not jumped out of the corral but into the barn, right over the three-and-a-half-foot door.

"He just loves hay," Renna sighed. "Look at his hay belly!" Pepper stared contentedly at her from his hay pile. "You need more exercise," she told him sternly.

Exercise is a must for your horse—not just a little exercise now and

No amount of grooming will give your horse a beauty you love to feel if worms are getting half his feed.

The freedom of a corral, regular riding, or some form of exercise is a must for your horse. When the mist sifts over the mountains, when horses graze nearby, when shade and sunshine mingle, when grass is green and lush, a horse has happiness. Give him a share of his natural world wherever you are.

then, but a regular diet of it. Muscle tone and looks depend on it.

The harder your horse works, the more you need to groom him. Domestic horses everywhere eat more than wild horses. The extra food makes them sweat more, accumulates more wastes on their skin, and just plain makes them dirtier. The more a horse works, the more you up the grain ration; the more you up the grain ration, the more you need to clean him. Every day he works he must be groomed.

His tack is important, too. He cannot have a well-groomed look if he has sores where tough, dry leather cuts up his flesh. A blanket or pad under the saddle helps.

Happiness for your horse. Perhaps it is not a must for the well-groomed look, but it can help. Picture what he has when he grazes on a broad plain, the sun making dapples on his coat, the wind lifting his mane a little, a half-dozen horses nearby, and always something to watch, from the birds pecking for bits of grain to the pattern of clouds on the horizon. How much of this can you give him? Let him see the world around him through the window of his stall. Let light and fresh air into his home. Give him companionship. Did you know you satisfy his need for a friend much the way another horse does? Of course, he does like another horse around, too, but sometimes he can't have everything.

9
Getting Ready to Groom

Do you always lead him on the left? No. That gate can bang him on his right side. You walk on the right side and hold the gate for him. (This wily Iceland pony swished his hip around so that the gate never banged him at all, but your horse might not know that trick.)

If your horse is in pasture, come quietly to him, no hand raised, no lead rope swinging in anticipation. An arm around his neck, then clip the lead to his halter. If he is in a stall, back him out . . .

... tie him with a horseman's knot that pulls out easily for you. The end can be tucked through so that it does not pull out easily for your horse.

If your horse wiggles and stomps, if he nips in play or bites a bit once in a while, tie his head snugly or else cross-tie him. Attach a rope to the ring on either side of his halter. When he has learned to stand still and discovered he can trust you, drop the ropes in front of him. Finally, he will get along without a rope at all.

Part II
GROOMING FROM HEAD TO HOOF

10

Where to Start

Cool. Dry. Feel between his forelegs to be sure. Only then can you groom him.

The left side. You begin there. Same place, same way, every day. Curry first from his ears to his shoulders, then follow up with the brush.

Umm. It feels good when you scratch right down to the crest.

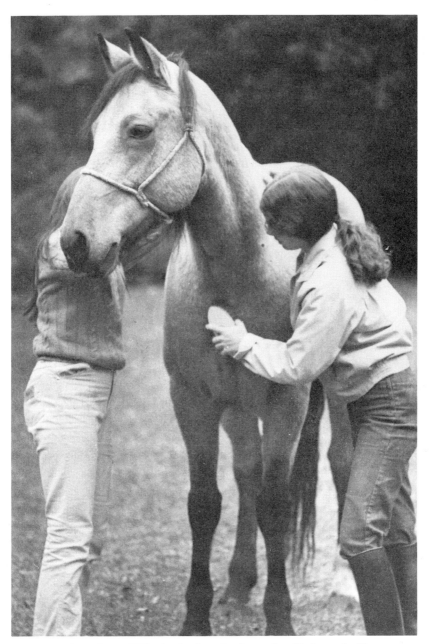

Clean his chest. Whisk the brush through all those hollows.

Easy with the curry between his front legs. You want it clean, but he's tender there. A hand on your horse tells you what he's doing. It also lets him know where you are, how you feel. Always touch him when your back is turned. If he moves, you'll feel it. Maybe he's curious, maybe it's something else he has in mind.

58

From his shoulder to his legs, make it sleek.

You forgot your brush? If you must go in front, hold him while you pass. You really don't want a bump from his big head.

11

Forelegs

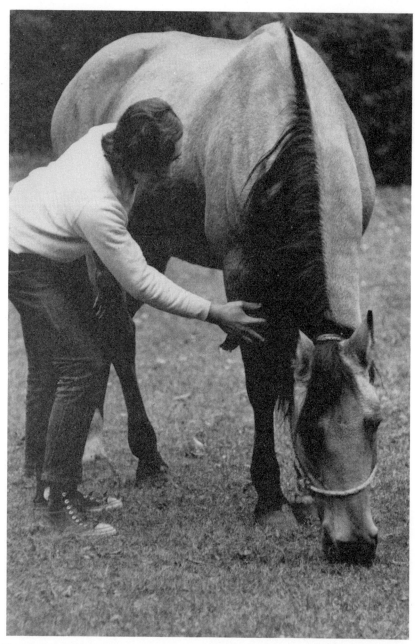

Bend over, don't stoop, when you clean a horse. Stay off your knees.

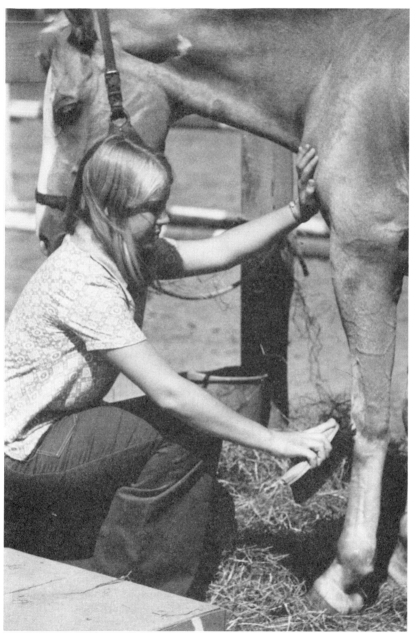

The currycomb's all right on his upper legs, but starting at his knees—brushes only please. Let mud dry before you brush it off.

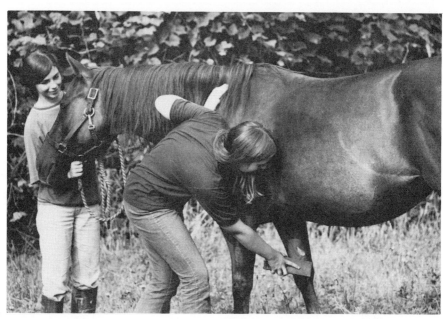

Legs are special. That's where his bones hug the skin. "Don't bang his bones," a camper wrote. "It hurts." Brush the inside of the leg you can see.

Down at the bottom, just above his hoof, where you'd think he ought to have an ankle, is his pastern. It is tender. So scrub back and forth in that groove. Be sure the bristles get down to the skin. Does it feel silky soft now?

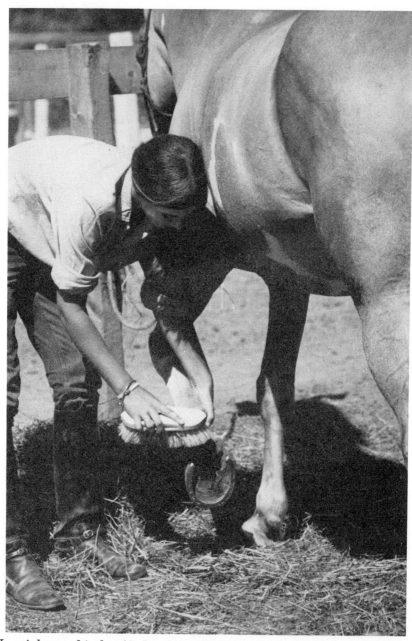

He picks up his hoof? Let him. Hold it firmly while you brush the pastern. Talk to him. Comfort him. Soon he'll stop fussing about the whole thing and keep his foot down. Brush the feathers, too. Those are the hairs behind his pastern. They are his mudcatchers.

12

The Middle:
Withers to Tail

*Curry and brush the withers (the big bone) and along the sides of it.
Easy on top where the bone is close to the surface. You want it really
clean lest the saddle rub a sore in the dirt you left behind.*

Clean his back, his sides. The side he sleeps on may be dirtier than the other. If you're in a hurry, clean the dirty side first. Go under his belly. Did he lift a foot or look at you angrily? Maybe he's ticklish underneath. If he is, just use your brush (no curry).

69

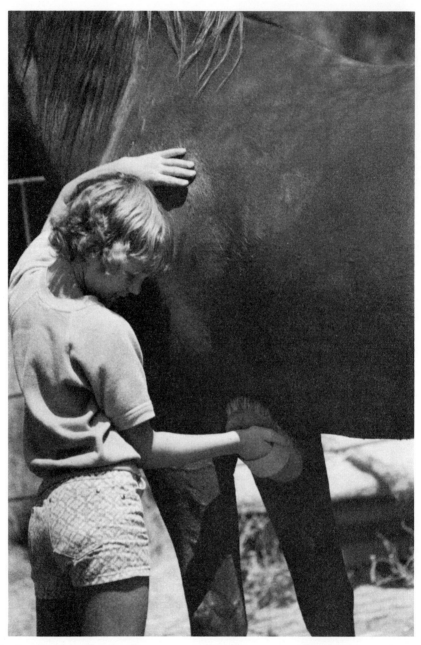

Right back of his forelegs is an important spot. Brush back and forth in the folds of his skin. His girth shoves the skin around and pulls it tight when he stretches, so that a sore starts there if he's dirty.

Brush gently (don't use a curry) high inside his hind legs. He or she is tender there.

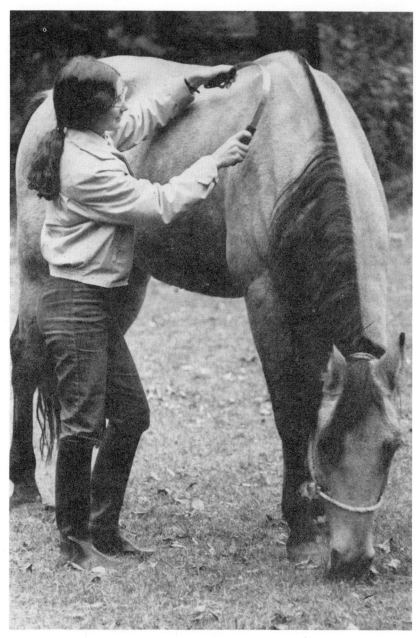

Loosen winter hair and scrape it away with the rough edge of the sweat scraper. A plastic brush works well, too.

13

The Hind Quarters

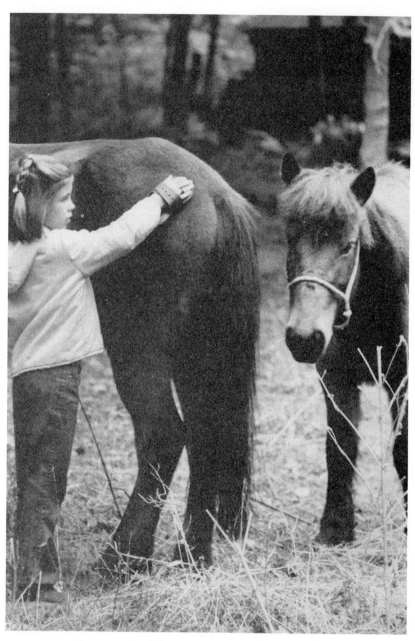

Rub and scrub his croup with a currycomb.

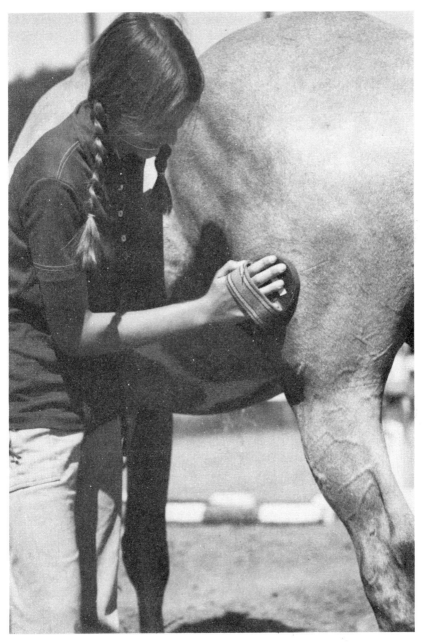

The upper part of his leg has flesh to cover the bones. Use a curry there . . .

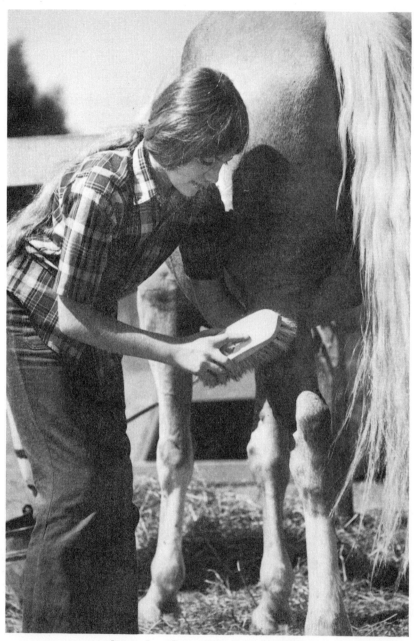

. . . then a brush, as you start downward.

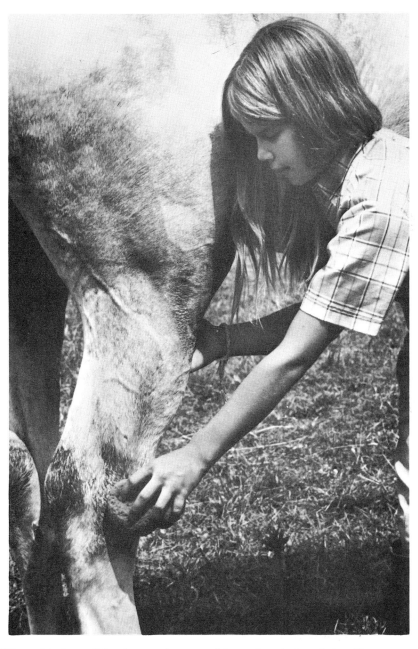

Those big-boned hocks can be a problem. A soft brush is all you use. If he is sensitive, use a sponge.

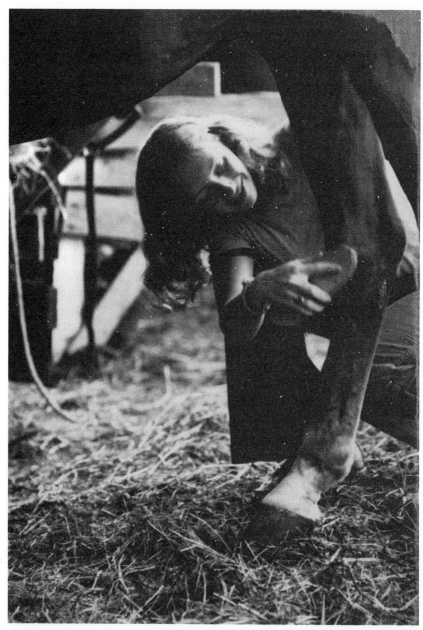

Don't duck under him. A horse can cow-kick—forward—with his hoof. You wouldn't want to be in the way. Remember the insides of his legs.

Hold his tail aside to clean the fleshy part of his legs there.

Clean the dock with a sponge.

Clean under his tail with a rag or sponge. Don't use the same rag for his face.

14

The Other Side

Pass close to him when you go behind his rump. Then his hoofs won't hurt; even if he kicks, his hocks just bump you. Speak to him as you go around. Ask a horse to move over. Don't push or be rough or loud.

Begin again by his ears.

Brush and curry thoroughly under his mane. He gets dirty there, too,
even if you don't see it. Now do as fine a job on this side.

15

His Head

Go over the bumps and hollows around his eyes. Go about it quietly, because he doesn't like big objects coming at his eyes in a reckless fashion.

Don't miss the poll, up there between his ears.

You can wipe his face with a rag instead of using a brush. A rag is a bit less fearsome, and his face isn't too dirty anyhow.

Wipe his lips and around his ears.

A sponge that isn't too wet will wipe the corners of his eyes.

Gently rub your sponge downward on the outer part of his nose.

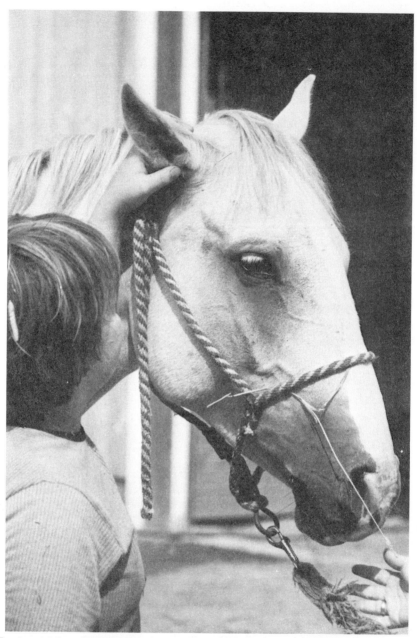

How sensitive those ears are! Rub your thumb up the inside to clean out any dirt that might have gathered in the hairs. Your fingers are even more gentle than a rag or sponge because you can feel just what you are doing and won't rub too hard.

What's she doing? Holding his tongue out the side of his mouth. "Like this, you animal!" she says. That way she can look at his mouth safely to see if his teeth need to be floated (ground down so that they meet evenly).

16

The Sheath

A stallion or gelding is not so sensitive on the sheath that you must leave him alone. It is an area you clean whenever it needs it.

Brush gently along the sides of the sheath.

Sometimes you should clean inside the opening of the sheath. Wipe it out with your fingers or an elephant ear sponge. Run your fingers around just inside the loose skin to wipe out any dirt that has collected there.

If your horse is not used to having his sheath cleaned, be alert the first few times you do it until you prove to him that he can trust you.

17

The Mane

"His mane is always growing on the wrong side," Kathy said. Sure enough, when we looked at his pictures through the years, his mane grew naturally on the left. For a hunter, this was all wrong. "I put braids in his mane to get it to stay on the right side," Kathy went on, "but as soon as I took them out, his mane flopped back again. At the riding club they used wave set when they put braids in and left them for a whole week. That worked."

You want style? Keep his mane even. But don't use scissors! You pull a mane. This means you pull out the longest hairs a few at a time until the mane is the length you like. This doesn't hurt him.

You don't mind someone pulling a couple of hairs on your head if he does it quickly, and you feel it a lot more than a horse does. He has a few nerves in his crest, though, so don't yank out a fistful at once.

Some horses have a full mane and tail. Working horses in the West have roached manes; and if you ride Western, you should follow the convention for the type of horse you own. (See section on horse shows.)

If your horse's mane becomes tangled, work with small sections at a time. Untangle the hairs, one or two at a time, with your fingers, then brush a bit. Begin at the ends and work upward.

Western horses often have roached (clipped) manes. (Choc Mool, ridden by Scott Wilson. Photo courtesy of J. I. Wilson.)

Keep his mane smooth and soft by daily brushing. You can use one of your old hair brushes, a dog brush, a mane brush, or a mane comb. If he has snarls, begin at the ends and work upward a little at a time. A brush pulls out less hair than a comb. Brush it until it is well separated, then brush a small section at a time until you've finished the whole mane.

Brush the mane over to the wrong side to get the underside of it.

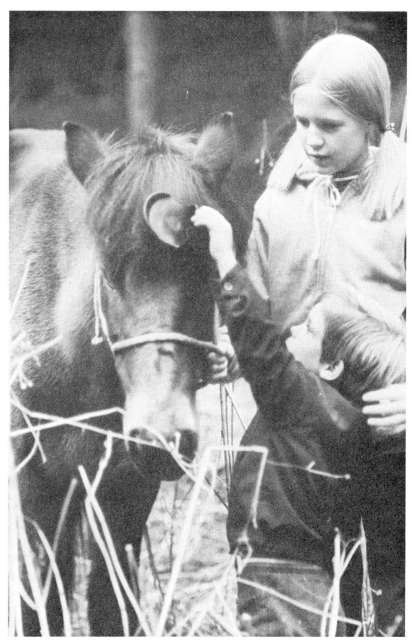

The forelock should be neat, too.

A horse's mane should fall to the right (the off) side. Brush it that way every day. If it is stubborn, dampen it with your brush to help it flop where it is supposed to go.

If it sticks up like a cow-lick, paste it with a mud pack to plaster it down. The mud will brush out easily after it has dried and done its job.

Braids train a mane to stay down and on the proper side. Take them out for brushing every couple of days.

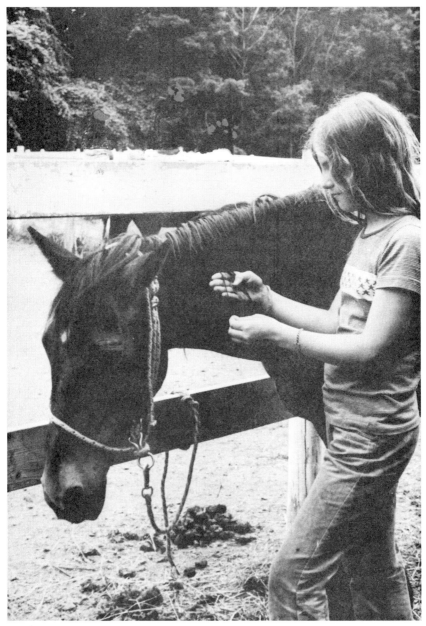

To thin a mane, pull the hairs from the underneath rather than those on the surface.

103

Pulling a mane: The more you pull it, the shorter it gets. When it is right, it will be smooth and even. Pull a few hairs each day; don't try to do the whole mane at once. First comb the mane flat. Then divide it in bunches; take the longest hair in the bunch. Shove the other hairs out of the way; give a quick pull to the long ones.

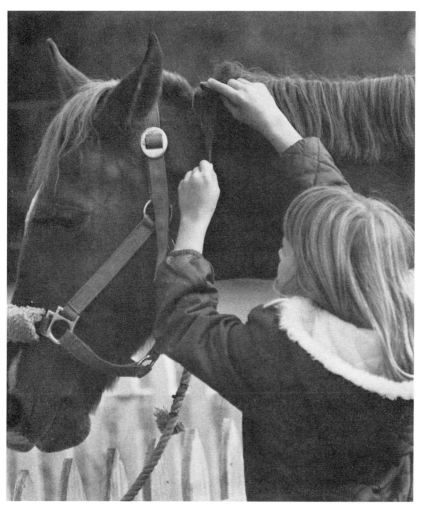

If you use a comb for pulling the mane, push up the short hairs with the comb (hang on to the long ones), then pull down sharply with the comb. You can loop long hairs around the comb, which saves your fingers, but most people find fingers work easiest for a smooth, natural look.

18
The Tail

Brush his tail, a little at a time. Hold up a bunch of hair with one hand while you brush upward and then downward with the other.

You can hold the whole tail with one hand as you drop a small section at a time for brushing with the other hand.

If you use a comb, take care not to rip out too many strands. Begin at the ends and work upwards.

The way to get out the snarls is little by little, separating the strands with your fingers, brushing a little, untangling a little bit more. Burs! A little baby oil helps with the untangling. Then you won't need to cut them out with scissors.

19
Hoofs

It is easiest to clean all four hoofs when you've finished the rest of your horse. Always go in the same order. The routine, in time, should teach him to pick up his feet for you and hold them up while you clean them.

The teaching process, like so much of grooming, is a matter of trust and routine. As your horse gets to know you will not hurt him, he becomes more willing to cooperate, even with his feet. Besides, you do it every day, often twice a day, and even if he argues with you about it, he knows you are going to win. Pick his feet up several times a day when you are teaching him to be willing about it. Praise him; pat him. Put his foot down, then pick it up again. Do this day by day and he'll learn.

It really isn't tricky to clean hoofs. The scary talk about hurting a horse refers to just one part of his hoof: the frog. The frog is the V-shaped part in the middle of his foot. A horse stands on the frog—it is his shock absorber—so it isn't so sensitive you can't even touch it.

When you hold a horse's hoof, don't twist it or move it into an awkward position so that you hurt him.

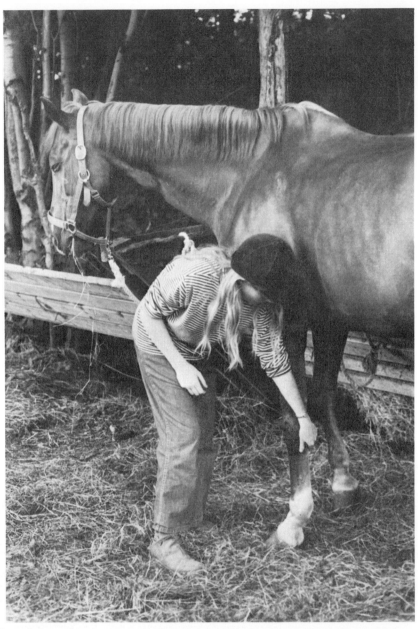

To ask for a hoof: run your hand down his leg beginning above the knee. Tell him, "Pick up," or any other word you want to use. When your hand is on the fetlock, give an upward pull.

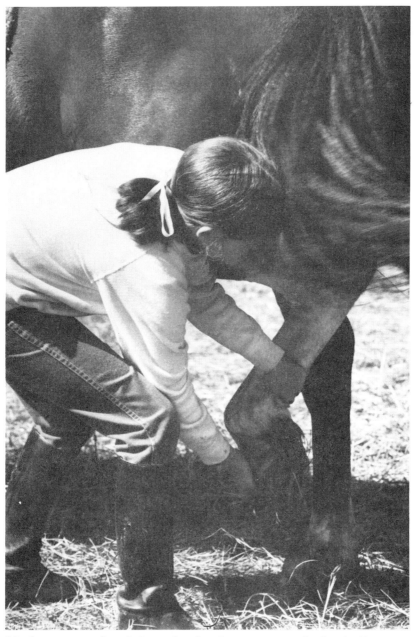

Behind: run your hand down his leg beginning at the hock. Be sure to stand beside him, not behind him.

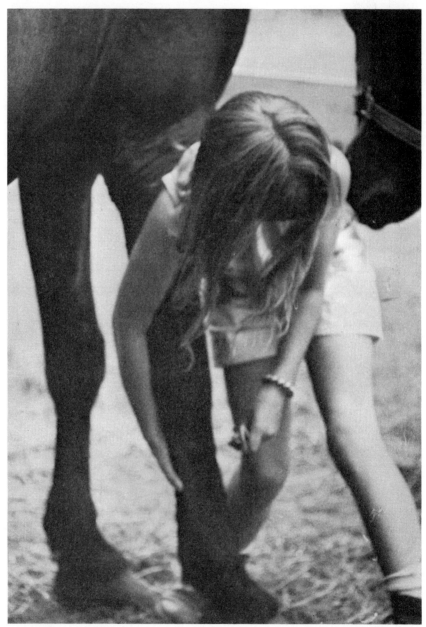

If you have trouble making him pick up his hoof, lean against his shoulder as you pull upward (this shifts his weight off that foot), or squeeze the tendon and press your arm behind his knee to bend his leg.

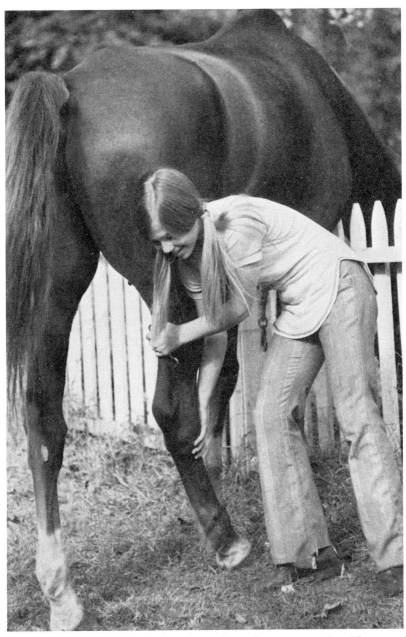

From behind, lean against his haunch—where your shoulder touches him. Or squeeze the large tendon just above the hock. Be ready to grab his foot and pull his leg out to the rear. Don't pull his leg to the side because it makes him lose his balance.

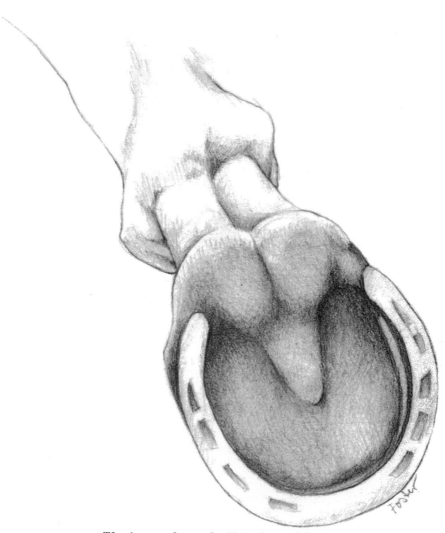

The frog—there, the V in the middle.

If he tries to put his foot down, hold it tight. Brace it underneath with your hand. Bend the fetlock joint sharply. Clean the toe part first, up around the circle of his hoof, away from the frog. Hold the hoof pick so there's not a chance of jabbing him, even if he moves suddenly.

Scrape the whole sole of his hoof. You can rest his hoof or his leg on your thigh.

You can hold his hoof between your legs if it is easier to keep a grip on it there. Don't uproot the shoe: that is, don't catch the hoof pick under it and yank it loose.

It is best to clean from the heel toward the toe in case he puts his foot down suddenly. You're less likely to jab the frog from that direction. An unshod horse needs his feet cleaned too. He will also need trimming.

Put his foot down for him. Don't just drop it.

Check his shoes every day. Tuck your hoof pick just a tiny bit into the edge of his shoe to see if it is loose. A loose or dangling shoe must be pulled. You don't want the shoe ripping off part of his hoof when it goes, or clanging him in the leg.

122

Hoof dressing or oil keeps hoofs moist. It's especially nice for your horse in summer. Give his hoofs a shine. It's a kindness to old horses, such as this one, who would let you lie under her feet.

123

Strong odor in his feet? Thrush! A fungus that starts when he stands in the wet. Kill it with bleach, straight from the bottle. Bleach can be kept in a plastic dishwashing liquid bottle. Or use bleach on a rag or sponge pressed hard against the sole of his foot. Best of all, keep his stall dry.

20
Finishing Touches

*Smooth the chestnuts. Those rough bumps inside his legs can be smooth.
Peel them off a bit at a time with your fingernail.*

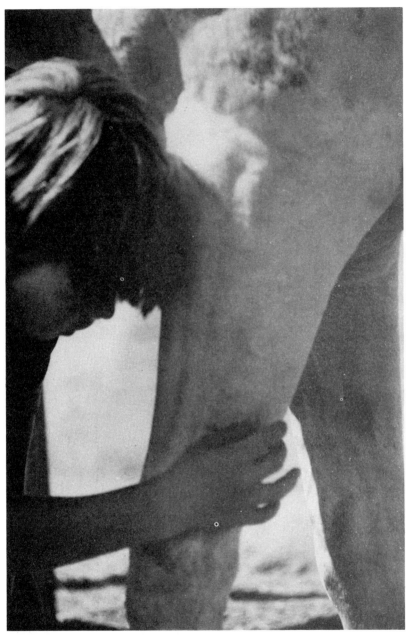

Yellow specks on his legs that defy the curry. Those are botfly eggs. In summertime they breed. Pick them off with your fingers . . .

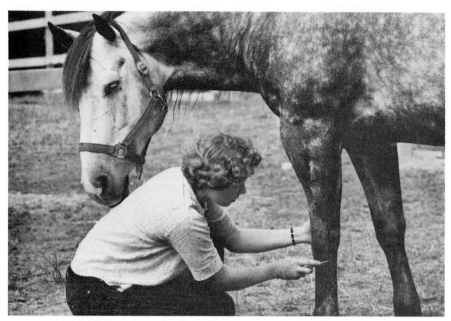

... or scrape them off with the edge of a knife if you are an expert with it, as this 4-H Club girl is. Or try a medium grade of sandpaper that you rub along his leg with the grain of his hair. Go easy though; you're only after the eggs, not his legs.

A hand-rub all over. It gives him a shine.

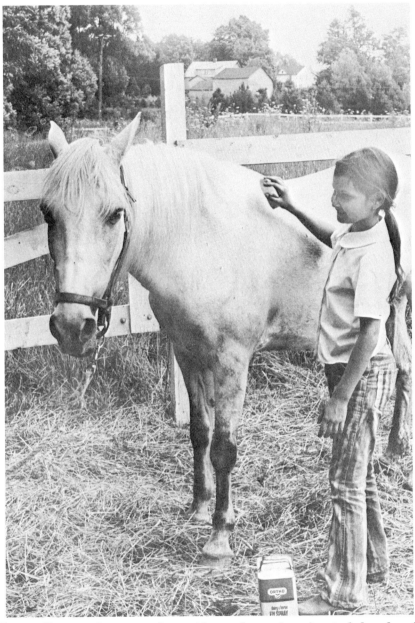

Fly repellant can be sprayed on—if your horse doesn't mind the whooshing sound—or wiped on with a sponge.

How can you tell if he's clean? Feel his coat. It should have the soft feel of velvet, the silky touch of an oriental hanging.

If you scratch with your nails, do you see lines of gray? Dandruff? Do your finger tips get dirty? Check the out-of-the-way places, so often missed: under the belly, inside legs and thighs, in the bends of the knees and hocks, below the ears, the pasterns.

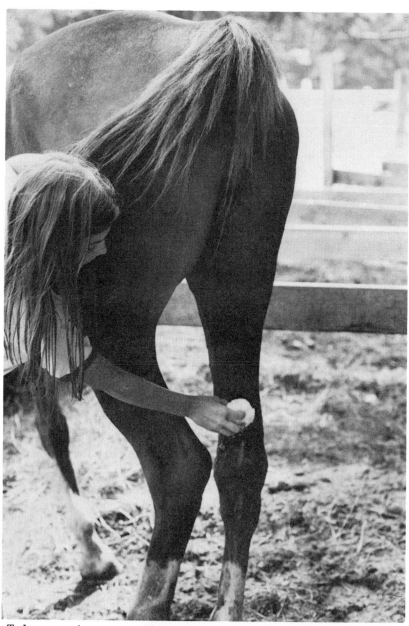

Take care of any cuts. Clean them with a bit of cotton—carefully.

Part III
SPECIAL FEATURES

21
Baths

You're ridden along a winding stream on a hot summer day. You've felt the tug on the bit, noted the arched neck, watched how eagerly your horse looked at the water. How much he wanted to lie down and roll! What fun to swim! It's the easiest bath to give.

A creek bath—for everyone. Start at his head, up between his ears. (Don't get water in his ears.) Go over his foretop and face. Follow the route you take when grooming: neck and chest, withers and shoulders, back and belly, and finally his legs. If you use shampoo, work it into a lather against the grain of his hair. Be sure all the shampoo floats away and none is left in his coat.

Did you know it can help a horse's feet to stand in the water a while once or twice a week? When he works hard, he sometimes gets sore feet. Give him a foot bath.

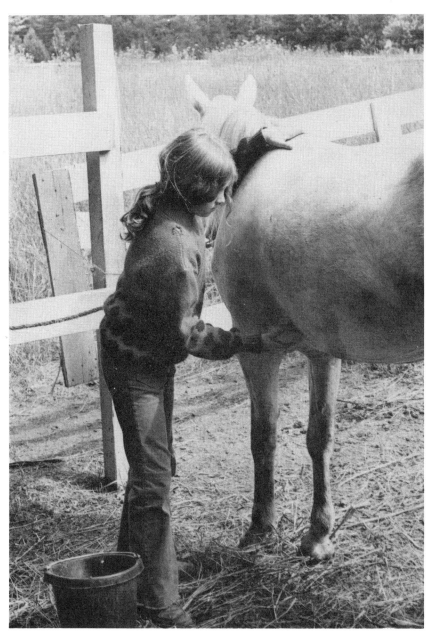

A bath with bucket and sponge. Don't forget the rinse. A little lanolin in the water will put the oil back in his coat.

Time for the sweat scraper. Go with the hair. Watch how the water drips away. (Don't use it on his head and legs.) Finish with a sponge to sop up what's left.

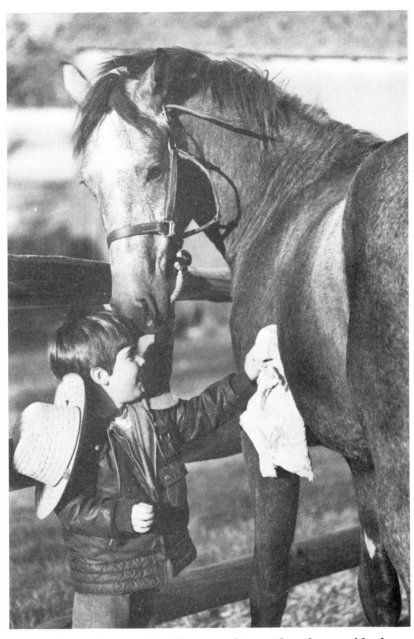

Rub him dry with a rag. Finally, cover him with a sheet or blanket until the dampness is all gone. In winter, unless your barn is warm and draft-free, he'll have to manage without a bath. If you really need to give him one, you can wash a small section at a time, dry it thoroughly, and then do another small section. You must do only a little at a time and there must be no drafts. Blanket him afterwards.

Shampoo for his mane. Any dog shampoo will do. His mane and tail need it the way your hair does—though not quite as often. Rub deep with your nails, right down to the crest. Rinse.

140

Sponge the shampoo on at the top of his tail, then dunk the whole thing in a bucket. Swish it around. Snap it dry.

Salt toughens the skin. A salt bath for the saddle and girth areas, especially in summertime, cuts down on girth and saddle sores. It helps with a thin-skinned horse, too.

22

Trimming

"I clip everything—ears, pasterns, everything," a veteran groom said emphatically, as he ran the clipper up the inside of a horse's ear.

"Leave it nature's way," another old-timer with horses said to me. "Nature put long hairs on a horse's leg to protect the pastern, so you ought to leave them there."

The first spokesman groomed horses at one of the finest riding schools in Connecticut. Several rings, several jump courses, and several barns stood amidst immaculate fields. A large indoor ring made winter riding comfortable, not just for riders but for horses who had been clipped as well.

The second spokesman lived in the country where most people kept their horses in barns always left open to corrals and fields in which the horses roamed outdoors in the snow in the winter and grazed in the summer.

The concern about fetlocks (whether you clip or don't clip) stems from the tenderness of the pastern. The long hairs on the fetlocks protect the pasterns. If you are uncertain which course to take, do as one horseman advises: leave some hair to give protection; clip some to make it neat. If you ride in shows, the decision is made for you: clip.

The same discussion arises about ears. In summertime, especially, the long hairs inside a horse's ear screen out dust and insects. You can clip the long hairs; you can clip the edges of the ears; you can clip the hair inside the ears. You can choose nature's way or the neat way. The decision is most likely to depend on how much show riding you do.

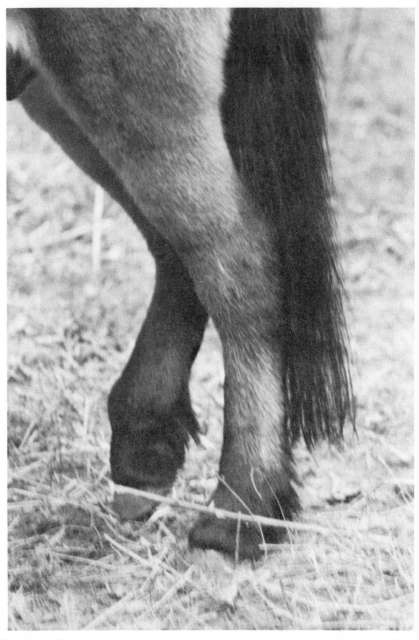

Untrimmed fetlocks give a horse's pasterns protection from mud and cold.

Trimmed fetlocks have the neat look. Fetlocks can be trimmed with scissors or with clippers. Clippers are easier; they cost more. Gradually edge off the hair so that there are no ridges.

You can trim the hairs on his ears without taking all the hairs out of the inside. Trim the edges by folding his ear in half the long way and cutting off all the hairs that stick out.

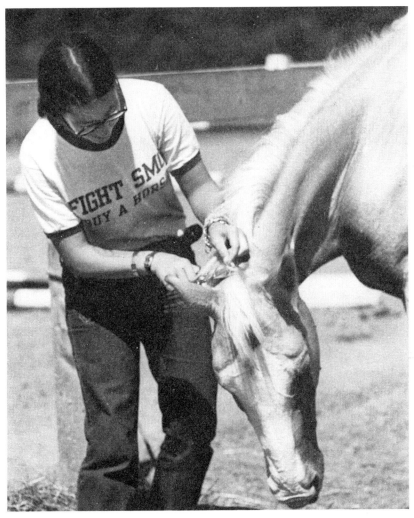

A bridle path. Clip a strip an inch wide (some riders clip it three inches wide) behind the ears. Clip right down to the crest, but leave the hair long at the edge of the bridle path.

The mane on a Quarter Horse or any roping horse is usually shaved off. Clippers make it easy. It is nice to leave a tuft of hair at the base of the mane as padding under the saddle.

23
Winter Clipping

You may wonder why the horses at most stables have all that soft winter coat clipped off their bodies. It isn't because their owners feel elite or are showing off their superior horses. Horses are clipped because they get hot. That thick winter coat acts like an insulating blanket to hold in all the sweat and heat when you ride. And it dries out ever so slowly. You just cannot put a horse in a drier.

If you clip off a horse's winter coat shortly after it comes in late in October or November, and again around Christmas or New Year's, keep him warm with a blanket. The blanket not only acts as a substitute for his coat when the sleet pounds the stable roof and snow piles outside the windows, but it slows down the growth of new hair.

Leslie Castle patted her horse's neck where his coat already showed a thickening for winter. "It grew more just in one night when I didn't put a blanket on him," she moaned. "It was so warm last night I thought he didn't need it. From now on he gets a blanket every night no matter what the weather is." She didn't want to clip him because he was out most of the day—by preference, for he had a barn he could use—but she didn't want a shaggy coat on him either.

If you plan to try clipping, think twice about it. In the first place, clippers are expensive. Once you've used them they are second-hand and hard to sell. In the second place, it is difficult to clip a horse. Lt. James Wilson, who shows successfully and does his own clipping, says, "It's a real task to clip a whole horse. You have to cover his entire body without missing a spot. Even with a good horse who stands, it's hard."

Lt. Wilson cuts down on the amount of clipping he has to do by feeding corn. The corn builds body heat, which in turn sweats out a horse's heavy coat. (It also helps keep a horse fat in winter.)

It takes several clippings to get any good at it; you'll get exasperated, discouraged, and impatient. If you are still determined to do it, buy good clippers, not the cheapest pair. Not only will you save yourself money because you are clipping your horse yourself, you'll save agony too. Good clippers clog less often; they need repair less often; they work better. Two pairs of clippers makes the task easier: one for the body, a small one for the head. The small pair makes less noise, can squeeze into the crannies better, and will be cool when you start on his face, because you haven't used it yet. Follow the instructions that come with the clippers for oiling them. Oil keeps the blades sharp, so don't disregard that part of the directions. Be sure to clean them thoroughly afterwards.

Remember, there's no law that says you have to clip the whole horse in one day. Do the easy part first if he is in a bad mood. Catch him on a calm day for his head and ticklish spots.

Do you have to clip your horse in winter? No. In cities and towns all over the countryside where the cold creates heavy coats in horses, you'll see healthy horses with thick hair stomping about in fields and beside barns. Most riders with backyard horses let nature take her course.

With a heavy coat for protection your horse can tromp the fields with glee come wind or snow. Just remember that any hard work is going to sweat him up far more than it does in summer. The surface hair will dry quickly, but always feel for the damp that lies underneath. After you ride keep your horse blanketed and out of drafts until he is dry—even if it takes all day.

"They didn't clip all their horses in the old days," Teddy Wahl of Round Hill Stables in Greenwich, Connecticut, said to me one cold October afternoon. "I remember those big lumber horses that pulled loads of wood all day in winter. They just had straight stalls made from rough boards from the mill. There were big gaps between the boards. At night the horses came in ringing wet. The men put the horses right into the stalls and it never did them any harm. None of them were clipped, either."

"Do you leave any of your horses unclipped today?" I asked.

Mr. Wahl smiled and said, "All my horses are clipped."

A horse in a show has to be clipped. Much as you love the raggery, thick coat of your pet, it just won't do in a show. The judge will never give you a second look. The only exception is a show at your stable or in your neighborhood where you know everyone and every horse is unclipped.

The following photos show you the method used by a man who has clipped horses for 20 years.

If you clip a horse's legs, you should stretch his forelegs forward to get the elbow. This pulls the skin tighter so that you can clip around the corners and loose skin more easily. Do the outside of the leg first, then reach across and do the inside of the opposite leg.

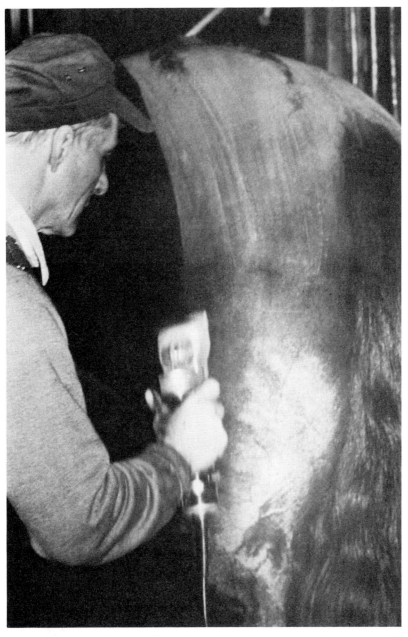

"*Just be patient,*" *says Don Cornell as he gives a four-year-old his first clipping. "That's all you really need to clip a horse: patience. If you do it right and don't get fussed, he'll trust you."*

Begin at the rear. "Why?" I asked, having read several books about it lately which said to start at the head. Don gave me a look as if I were as ignorant as I felt. "Because that's the way the hair goes. You clip against the grain of the hair." Note the diamond or triangle by the tail. One straight line on each side to a point over the tail—but close to it.

151

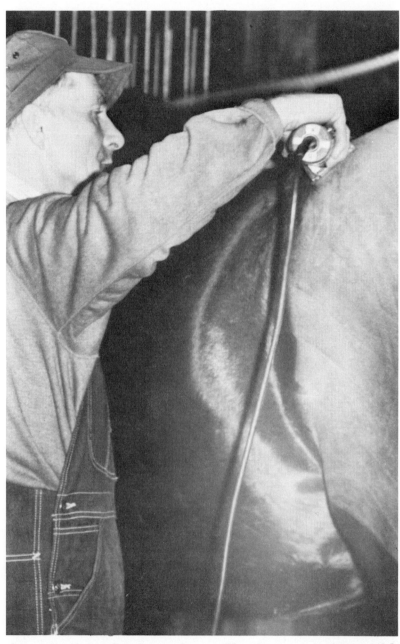

Light strokes do it. Overlap each one. The clippers run from tail head-ward across his croup and back.

"With a hunter, you don't clip the legs," Don said. He cut a smooth line across the top of the horse's leg. The line on his foreleg runs from the back of the elbow up to the front of the forearm. You see the natural dip in the flesh there.

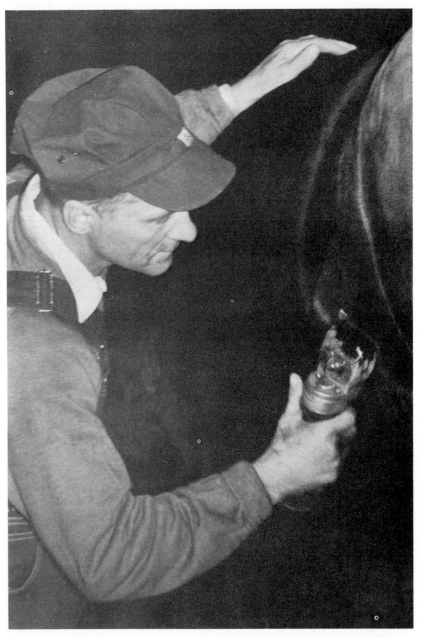

"The flanks are tender," Don said. "That's a spot to watch." The first strokes of the clippers go upwards along the flanks . . .

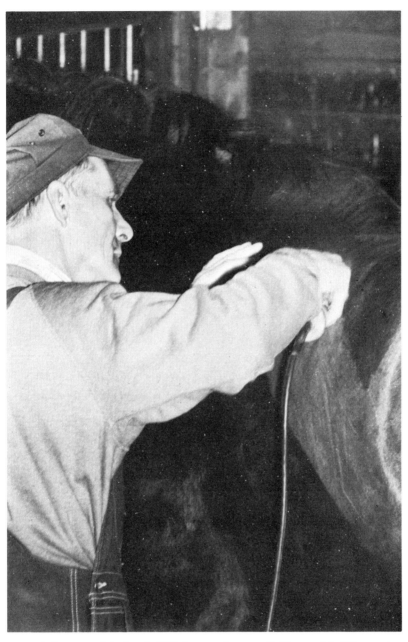

... *straight up to his back. "He's a quiet one," Don said. "Sometimes I get one that's been clipped for years and is so bad I have to knock him out. I'd rather have a horse who has never been clipped so that he's unspoiled by someone hurting him in the past."*

155

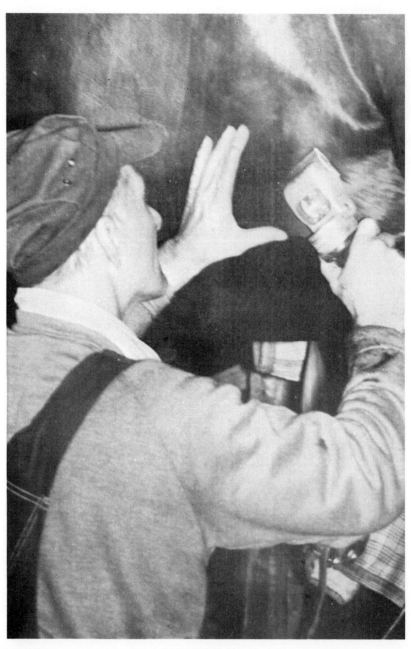

His belly is next. Clip along the sheath. That's where you have to be most careful," Don said. "It's about the tenderest spot. Mares too, the same way. "You got right down on your knees beside him," I commented." He smiled. "It's the only way you can get at him and see what you're doing."

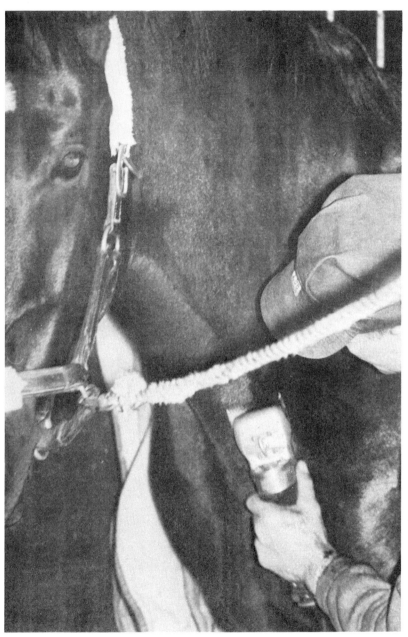

Get into the hollows on his chest.

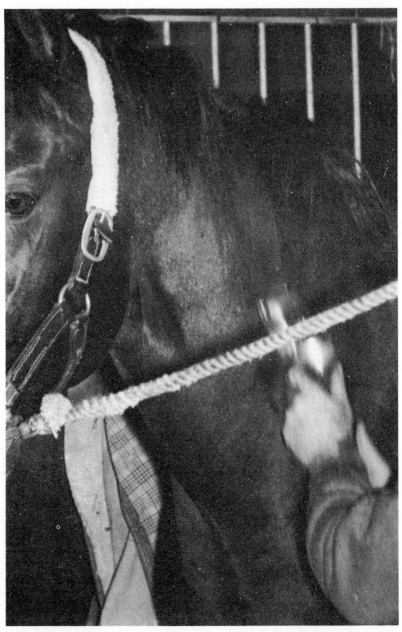

The strokes go up his neck toward the crest. Make a neat line with the edge of the clippers right at the crest on his neck. (Be sure all the mane is over on the other side when you cut the line.)

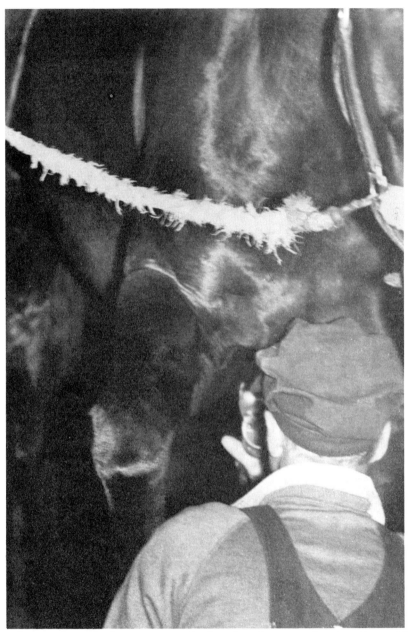

Bend your horse's knee to stretch the skin between his forelegs. "The other tender spot is in the folds of skin around his elbows," Don said.

The other leg will stretch the skin where it wrinkled before. An elbow under your horse's knee will keep his foot out of your face and his leg bent.

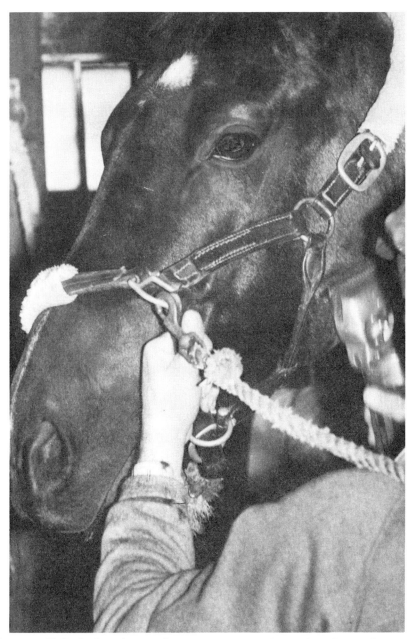

If you pull the halter forward, you can clip right to the edge of his face. The cheekbones are smooth and get you started on the face while you feel out how your horse will react. (Don is still using the big clippers, but he will switch to the smaller animal clippers, the size you use on poodles.)

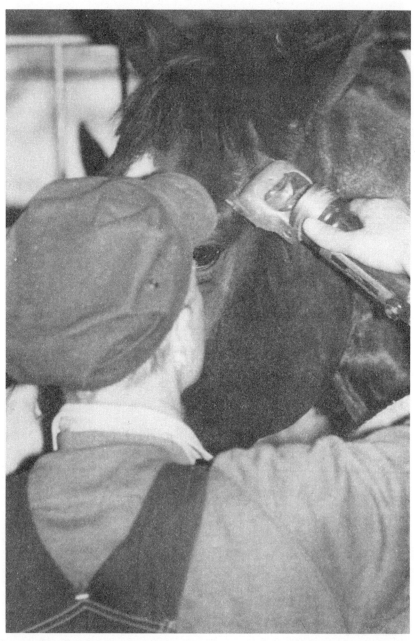

Across his forehead into the crannies and over the bumps around his eyes and brows. Trim the muzzle and whiskers with the small clippers.

Get behind the ears. "This colt is unusual," Don said. "Usually you need
a twitch to do his ears." The first time you use a twitch you feel nervous
about it. (A twitch can be made with a piece of broomstick or dowling
through which you bore a hole. Loop a cotton rope through it; knot it.
The smooth rope loop goes around the upper lip. Twist the stick until
the lop tightens just enough on the lip to hurt him a little. Then he for-
gets all about ears and clippers and you.)

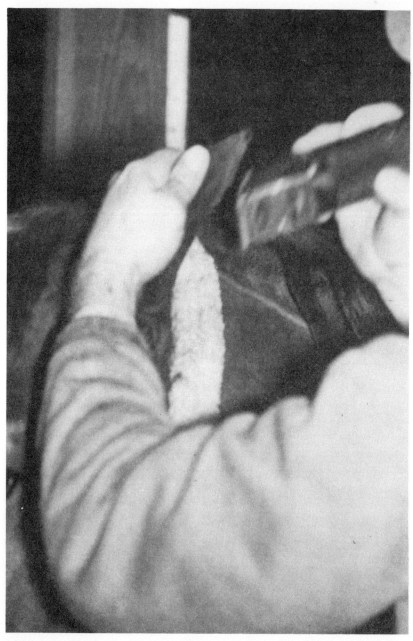

Fold his ear; cut the hairs along the front edges. Hold his forelock out of the way and his ear back. That should let you get the last rough hairs.

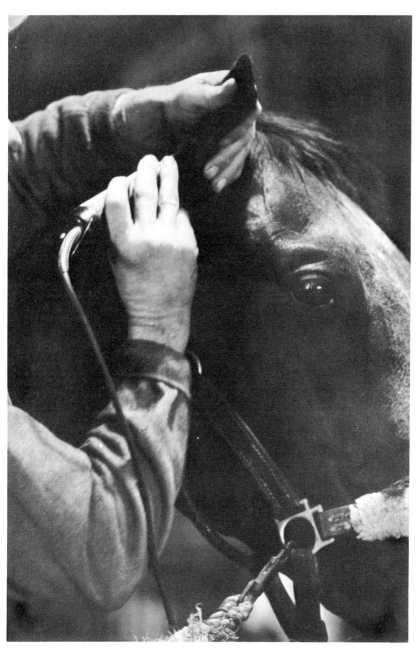

Clip right up his ear from the base to the tip. Do the inside the same
way with a couple of firm sweeps through the center of his ear. Once
over with a brush when you finish, then with a slightly damp sponge. A
horse who has just been clipped will feel a bit sore, so don't use a currycomb on him. Now as autumn steals away the golden leaves and winter
breathes its first cold breaths, there's a smartness still in your horse—
he's clipped.

24

Horse Shows— English and Western

Now is the time that understanding your horse pays off. "If you hope to win in a horse show, from 4-H to Madison Square Garden, one of the important prerequisites is to know your horse," says Joe Fargis, who was a member of the United States Equestrian Team when he was only 20.

A horse show! Just what do you have to do to groom your horse to perfection? You want him to shine. And maybe, just maybe, you'll win a ribbon.

His mane should be well combed, lying flat, trim and neat. In some classes you want a pulled mane. How long should it be? "Anywhere from one and one half to six inches," says one expert.

"I like it short so I can braid it when I want for English hunter classes," says another show rider.

"It should be even with his eye," one girl who shows often quoted her authority.

"As long as the mane comb," still another says.

If he is spotlessly groomed, will he win? It takes more than grooming. Remember the *musts* for a well-groomed horse? These help give him "that look."

There's more, too. A flabby horse who has had little exercise looks flabby among conditioned horses. He will probably sweat more than the other horses. And if he tires easily, well, you can guess what the judge thinks of a horse that pants!

Snip off his whiskers. ("By the very next day they had started to grow out again!" she sighed.) There's all the other clipping, too, whether you ride English or Western: his ears, fetlocks, coronets, and, in winter, his whole coat.

Whether you keep his mane pulled long or short, it should have the natural look. You must not cut it the way you do your hair.

Tails, too, should be neat and combed. Even a full tail should be pulled for proper appearance. Pull the hairs one or two at a time from underneath and the sides to give it a narrow look. Leave the hairs long on the dock; thin below the dock.

Remember all the little things and all the big ones. His hoofs, for example. They must not be peeling or cracked. Check his shoes before you van him. Rout out the blacksmith quickly if your horse needs help with his shoes.

Know your class. Read over the rules. Check the entrance requirements. Learn about the customs governing the class in your part of the country. Don't come into your class with a braided mane if your horse should have a full mane flowing free and soft to his withers. If his mane should be roached, don't come into the class after it has grown out a couple of inches.

169

White markings must look white to give that striking appearance that sets your horse apart from all others. They need to be washed the day of the show. Your whole horse may need a shampoo beforehand, but not on the day of the show. Once he is clean use a blanket or sheet to keep him that way.

Do not leave everything until the last day. Even braiding, if it is a slow, painstaking task for you, can be done the night before. On the day of the show your horse is going to sense the excitement around him, even if you are calm as a rock. You don't want to fuss him up more with too many last minute details.

Usually in English classes for working hunters you braid your horse's mane, thin his tail, and braid the dock or upper part of it. Yet at the National Horse Show in Madison Square Garden last year, two entries in one working hunter class had full manes and tails.

A judge in a hunter class was asked why competitors braided their horse's manes and tails. "It's not in the rule books," the judge said. "If most of the riders started entering classes without braids, the custom would end."

The rules are not inflexible. Arabian horses shown in classes in western New York State usually have their manes clipped to about four inches. Lt. James I. Wilson, whose daughter Susan recently won the New York State all-breeds performance championship in the under-eighteen division, has two Quarter Horses: one with a roached mane,

The three-gaited American Saddlehorse has a clipped mane and the first five inches of his tail shaved from the base. But the five-gaited Saddlehorse has a full mane and tail with only the foretop and the first lock of the mane braided.

In Western classes, Arabians are shown with full manes and tails. Usually Quarter Horses have roached manes and pulled tails.

one with a full mane. Both horses enter and win in Western reining and trail classes. Lt. Wilson has 180 ribbons for one season to prove this approach can't be all wrong.

What is causing this relaxation in custom and rules? It is due, partly, to the increased popularity of many pure breeds. The Quarter Horse is now shown both English and Western. A rider often wants to show his Quarter Horse in both types of classes. A roached mane, so necessary to cowboys who don't want to cut their fingers on long hairs while roping, looks most out of place in an English class. Sometimes a compromise is a pulled mane on a Quarter Horse that is shown in both types of classes, and judges in both styles of riding often permit it.

Double registrations can confuse the issue. Palominos, usually shown with full manes, can be Quarter Horses. You can have a registered Appaloosa that is also a Quarter Horse. The Appaloosa is a bit scanty in the mane and tail; sometimes the poll is clipped too. Ginger Trautwein, long familiar with the show ring as a rider and instructor of show riders, recalls a discussion about double registraton. "I've never seen a Quarter Horse that is a paint," she said.

A stranger overheard her and said, "I have a Champion Quarter Horse Paint."

Clipping is custom, too, but it does enhance the neatness of a horse.

172

But you can be a blue ribbon winner on an Arabian with a trimmed mane. (Ima Blond Too, ridden by Sue Wilson. Photo courtesy of J. I. Wilson.)

Western as well as English riders clip the winter coat. "I clip everything, for my Western horses just the same as for English," Lt. Wilson said. "That includes muzzle, pasterns, under the belly, ears, the works."

You may have to choose carefully the type of class you enter, but if you have the right horse and spend enough time on his conditioning and grooming, you can take part in the exciting competition of horse shows.

Remember, when the show is over, grooming is not. You need to take off his bandages and rub down his legs. You need to take out the braids.

25

Braiding the Mane

You will need to braid your horse's mane for the hunt and for some classes in the show ring. Brush it out first. Sometimes it helps to wet it slightly. If it needs to be evened, follow the instructions for pulling a mane in the chapter on manes.

You will do a better job of braiding if you do it the night before the hunt or the horse show. If your horse has a light mane, use brown thread or light-colored elastics. Thread holds much better than rubber bands do, but it takes longer. You will learn to do it well only with practice.

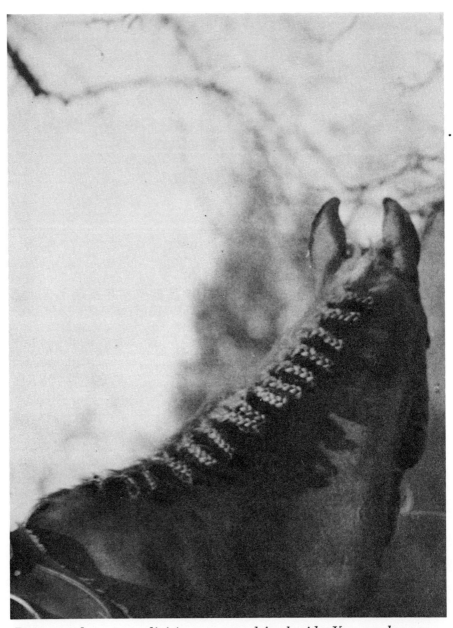

Figure out how many divisions you need for braids. You can have anywhere from 12 to 22 although 12 to 15 is usually enough. If your horse's neck is a bit long, use fewer braids so that his neck appears shorter. (Use a few more braids if he is short-necked.) The forelock is braided in one braid.

Divide out about one inch of mane for the first braid. (You may need as much as three inches if you make fewer braids.) Put a long bobby pin or hair clip on the next section of mane to keep it out of the way.

Braid tightly. Pull downward, close to the horse's neck. Put a rubber band on the end. (The small kind used for braces is just the right size.) If you really want it to stay, sew it. Wrap the thread around the tiny ends. Fold the ends under. Sew it again. Decorate his mane with wool yarn (threaded into a big needle). You can decorate a pony's mane or an open jumper's mane, but never a hunter's or an equitation class horse's mane. When the braid is finished, sew the yarn through the end. Fold the braid back on itself and sew through the top as close to the mane as you can get. Tie the ends of the yarn in a bow.

178

To sew the braid: double it under; sew through the top and middle. To make tiny button braids: double it under a second time; sew it. Note in the picture how two braids have come unsewed in the center. If you use rubber bands, take an extra twist or two in the braid after you fold it back. Keep the rubber band close to the crest.

The finished braid should be tight, lie flat on the neck, and not be full of prickly ends sticking out all over. The braids should be in proportion to your horse's neck. Use longer braids on a thick neck, small button braids on a thin neck.

26

Braiding the Tail

It is not difficult to braid a tail. Several methods are illustrated here. The first method is shown with a practice-at-home tail made out of cardboard and string. The second is with drawings. The third is with a horse's tail. No matter how you braid the tail, the top of it (the dock) is braided first.

The hair should be long on your horse's dock. Comb it out smooth as it can be.

Here is a make-believe tail. The white string comes from the back, the gray from the middle of the front of his tail. Take a strand from the back of his tail on either side. Cross them.

Pick up a strand from the middle of his tail. Braid them together.

Take a new strand from the back of the right side of his tail. You will need to combine two of the strands. If the center strand is thickest, count that as one. You can combine the remaining two in your hand, or you can cross the right hand one and then combine it with one that last came in from the left. It will fall naturally with the one from the left side. In this picture, you can see the two strands combined across the finger of the right hand.

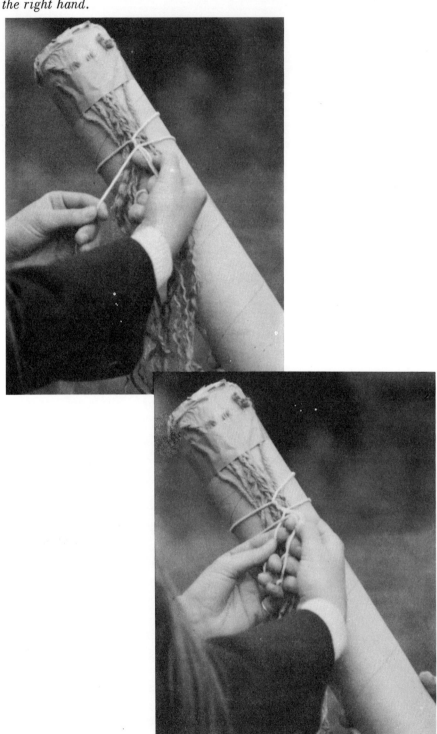

Pick up a strand from the left side of the tail. Braid it a couple of times. Continue picking up strands from alternate sides. Always keep three strands in your hand at one time.

With a horse's tail in front of you, you can try the following method which differs from the first one only in the way you start braiding.

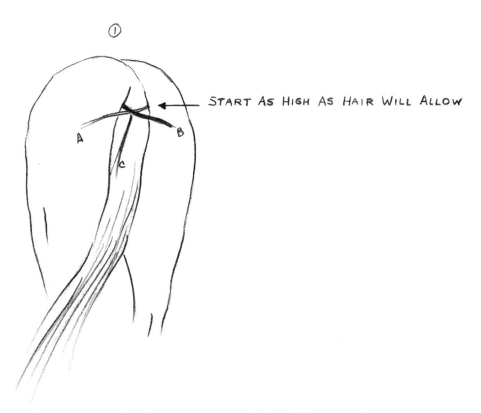

START AS HIGH AS HAIR WILL ALLOW

Pick up a strand of hair (about one inch width) from the back or right side of the tail and another the same size from the left side. Pull them to the center and twist them together. You may even knot or sew them together. Take a piece the same size from the center front, of the tail. Braid the three pieces tightly.

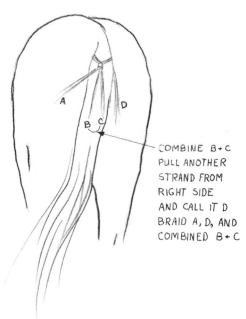

②

COMBINE B + C
PULL ANOTHER
STRAND FROM
RIGHT SIDE
AND CALL IT D
BRAID A, D, AND
COMBINED B + C

*Combine center and right pieces. (That leaves two pieces in your hand.)
Bring in a new section from the right. Braid it a couple of times with
the two in your hand. When you get good, you may braid each piece
only once.*

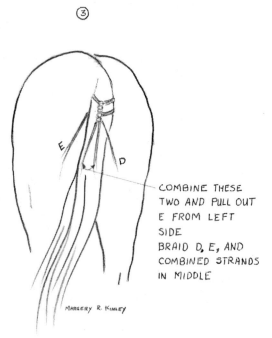

③

COMBINE THESE
TWO AND PULL OUT
E FROM LEFT
SIDE
BRAID D, E, AND
COMBINED STRANDS
IN MIDDLE

MARGERY R. KINLEY

*The original left strand is now short. Combine it with the center piece.
(If the hairs are too short for braiding, add a bit more from the center.)
Pull a new section from the left side. Braid it a couple of times. Add
alternate sections from the right and left sides and braid until you have
almost reached the end of the dock. Leave a couple of inches of bone
at the end.*

④

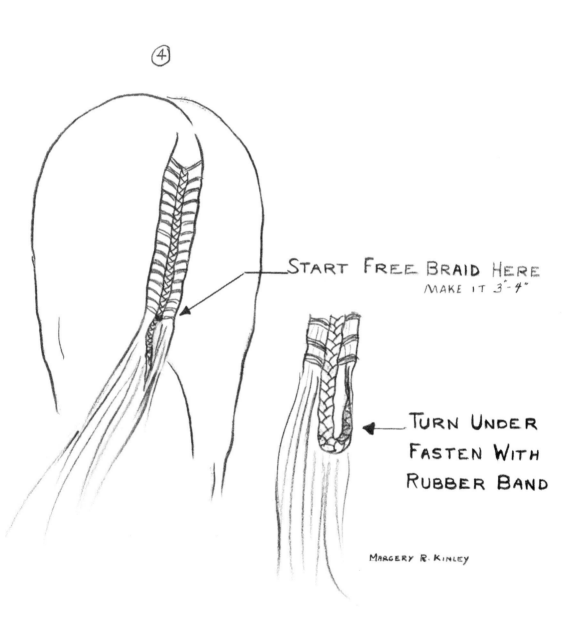

START FREE BRAID HERE
MAKE IT 3"-4"

TURN UNDER
FASTEN WITH
RUBBER BAND

MARGERY R. KINLEY

187

You will notice in these drawings that only a few inches of the tail are used in the thin braid below the dock. In the photograph, a much longer portion of the horse's tail is braided. Both methods are acceptable. You are looking for the neat, narrow, well-groomed look in his tail. The results, rather than the method, are what count.

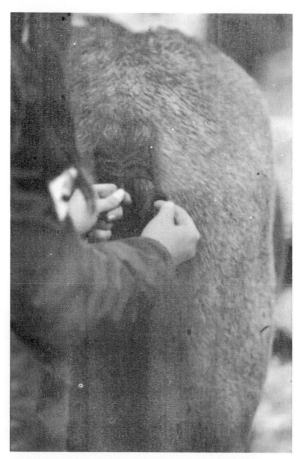

Note how a new piece is taken from the back side of the tail.

The braid gives a tight neat appearance to the top of the tail. Most of the hairs at the bottom of the tail are left to fly free. After you have finished braiding the dock part of the tail, pick up three sections of hair from the outer (front) part of his tail. These hairs will be long. The hairs you have left from the top of his tail are braided into these long hairs.

189

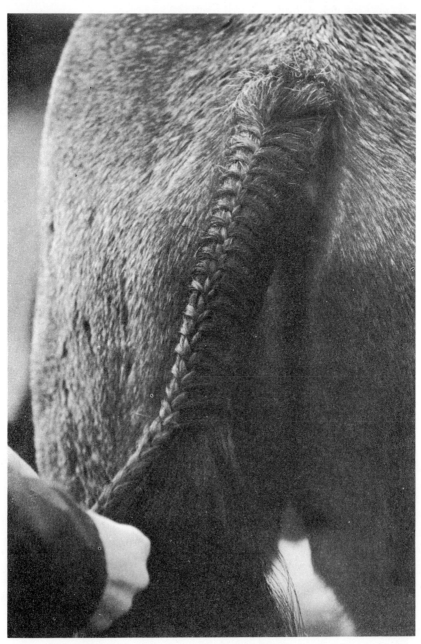

Braid the long strands right down to the tips.

*Put a rubber band on the end of the braid. Double the tiny ends under
and catch them in the rubber band. Fold your thin braid up to make a
loop. Fasten it with a rubber band. Tuck the thin braid up inside the
braiding on the dock. It will hold securely there . . .*

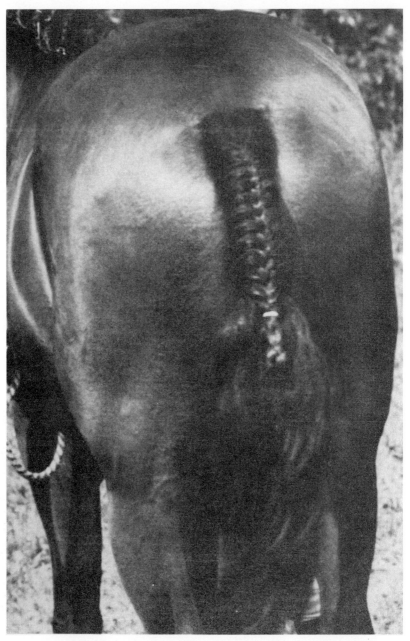

. . . or you can fold the braid behind itself, fasten it with a rubber band or thread, then fold it up behind itself a second time as you do a braid on his mane. For some shows you can let the thin braid dangle.

A mud tail is done a bit differently. After the dock is braided, braid all of the long hairs on the rest of his tail. Fold this lower section and tuck it up under the braided dock, and sew it in place. It, too, is permitted in a show.

A mud knot is one other method of finishing a tail. It protects the tail from getting dirty on a wet hunt course or on a muddy trail. Some people braid the top part of the tail before forming the knot. Usually, however, the knot is tied after simply spliting the long hairs on the tail below the dock.

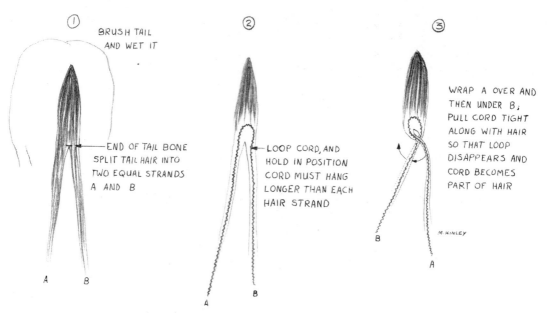

As you fold the knot, keep the twine to the inside so that it is covered by the hair.

Wrap the left section once all the way around the right piece.

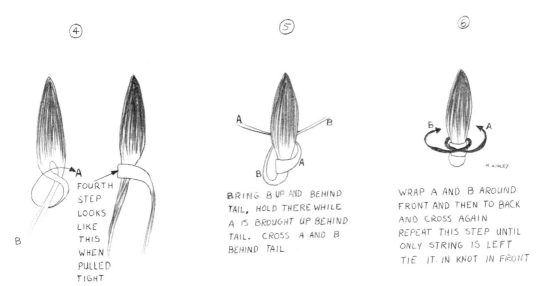

④
⑤
⑥

FOURTH
STEP
LOOKS
LIKE
THIS
WHEN
PULLED
TIGHT

B

A

BRING B UP AND BEHIND
TAIL, HOLD THERE WHILE
A IS BROUGHT UP BEHIND
TAIL. CROSS A AND B
BEHIND TAIL

A
B
B
A

WRAP A AND B AROUND
FRONT AND THEN TO BACK
AND CROSS AGAIN
REPEAT THIS STEP UNTIL
ONLY STRING IS LEFT
TIE IT IN KNOT IN FRONT

B
A

M. KINLEY

Wrap the pieces tightly. Alternate the two pieces. Wrap first one, then the other, crisscrossing them above the knot.

⑦

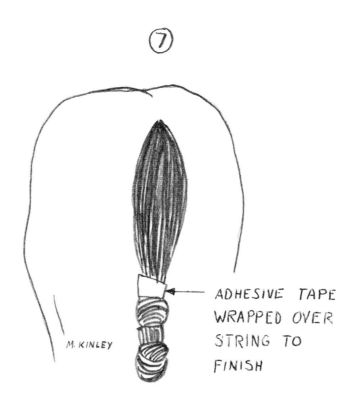

M. KINLEY

ADHESIVE TAPE
WRAPPED OVER
STRING TO
FINISH

195

What is important about braiding a horse's tail? Comb it thoroughly first. It helps to wet it slightly with a damp brush. Braid it tightly. When you bring in pieces from the side of the dock, stretch them tightly, but not so tight they pull out. Bring in the pieces as straight, horizontally, as you can. Right angles to the lines of the braid give it the best appearance. Don't let the braid sag in the middle, pulling down the hairs you've brought in from behind. Begin the braid as close as possible to the top of the tail. Make it long enough; two-thirds of the way down is better than half-way. You will need to practice and practice to braid well, but it is actually easier and faster to braid the tail than the mane, so don't get discouraged while you are learning.

Protect the tail for vanning or if you braid it the night before the show. Bandage it. An elastic type bandage for wrists is a good size and length. If you leave the long hairs you braided hang down, put them up under the bandage overnight.